ON OUR OWN

Other Books by Paul Dickson

Think Tanks
The Great American Ice Cream Book
The Future of the Workplace
The Electronic Battlefield
*The Mature Person's Guide to Kites, Yoyos, Frisbees and
    Other Childlike Diversions*
Out of This World: American Space Photography
The Future File
Chow: A Cook's Tour of Military Food
The Official Rules
The Official Explanations
Toasts
Words
*There Are Alligators in the Sewers and Other American
    Credos* (with Joseph C. Goulden)
Jokes

ON OUR OWN

*A Declaration of Independence
for the Self-Employed*

by Paul Dickson

Facts On File Publications /05387
New York, New York ● Oxford, England

On Our Own
A Declaration of Independence for the Self-Employed

Copyright © 1985 by Paul Dickson

Library of Congress Cataloging in Publication Data

Dickson, Paul.
    On our own.

    Bibliography: p.
    Includes index.
    1. Self-employed—United States. 2. Small
business—United States. I. Title.
HD8037.U5D53 1985   338.6'42   84-24734
ISBN 0-8160-1187-7
Published by Facts On File, Inc.
460 Park Avenue South, New York, N.Y. 10016
Printed in the United States of America

Composition by Facts On File/Circle Graphics
Printed by R.R. Donnelley & Sons Co.

10   9   8   7   6   5   4   3   2   1

CONTENTS

INTRODUCTION

The shift in the structure and character of work has created a demand that work produce more than purely economic benefits. To make a living is no longer enough. Work also has to make a life.

—Peter F. Drucker

To many people, breaking loose from the world of wages and salaries in favor of the riskier business of self-employment has become the preferred alternative.

Some have already done it, some are planning to do it and others wistfully and unrealistically dream of it. From all accounts, both the reality and aspiration have risen through the 1970s and continue to climb in the 1980s, reversing a downward trend which was more than a hundred years old. It was this dramatic turnaround which finally quieted those who saw self-employment as a dying anachronism with little chance of making it into the 21st century and gave inspiration to those who were never meant to be organization men and women.

This book is about the reality and the aspiration. It is not a conventional how-to book full of useful addresses and step-by-step instructions—there are a number of fine books of this type already in print—but rather a report which attempts to describe what has happened and, in the process, give an identity to the new cohort of American self-employed. Lest there be any question, the self-employed of the 1980s are a vastly different group than their 1960s counterparts who were, in large degree, aging outcasts of corporate society.

In describing this identity, I have drawn heavily on national employment trends as well as a survey I made of close to 200 self-employed people. Through interviews with these people I have attempted to get a hold on why people do make the break and why most of them would never, ever go back. And through a patchwork of odd statistics and facts I have attempted to set it all into the context of American life—a State of the Union report on the self-employed.

Fortunately, it is now possible to deliver such a report as government agencies (the Labor Department, the Internal Revenue Service, the Census Bureau and the Small Business Administration) are taking enough of an interest in this segment of the working population that facts not available a few years ago are now being developed.

Within this larger picture the book does not shy away from nuts-and-bolts considerations—taxes, pensions and emptying your own wastebaskets (one of the truly metaphoric distinctions between the self-employed and the employed, who generally have some other employee empty their trash). Nor does it avoid the politics of the subject, which are seldom discussed publicly but which are most important to the past, present and future of the state of self-employment.

It is also an intensely personal book written by one who has been on his own since September 22, 1969 and who is, at 45, still as excited by the freedom, risk and reward of self-employment as he was when he first converted at age 30. If there are moments in this book which make it sound like an adoring testimonial—a valentine—to the state of self-employment, so be it.

Lest there be any question about my bias in this matter, it is that self-employment is a matter of passion and ideology rather than a mere variation on the standard concept of going to work for somebody else. And though I work as a writer, I find that my own personal identity as a self-employed person is the stronger part of the way I see myself. I can honestly say that I have more in common with the self-employed in other fields than I do with employed journalists. I can't prove this, but I think that this happens to a lot of us after a few years on our own. There is a certain group identity at work here.

Finally, this book looks at self-employment as an American institution with a future. It looks at the future and examines the reforms and changes which could further brighten that future. It takes more than a passing glance at those major societal issues—ranging from new technology to the aging offspring of the baby boom—and their influence on self-employment. It dwells at some length on the odd collection of regulations which inhibit self-employment including one federal, 18 state and countless local laws that interfere with the right to work at home.

What I have attempted to do with all of this is to come up with the book I would have given anything to get hold of when I first made the leap and would have liked to have had in the years since. In that same spirit, the book is intended for those who have been at it for a while as well as for those who are contemplating the prospect of becoming their own boss.

If nothing else, it shows that going on your own has become a powerful element in American life and an emerging economic force. If there is "news" in this book, it is that we are no longer a mere demographic novelty but a wonderfully motley economic force which, among other things, has been given a disproportionately large share of the job of refinancing the Social Security system and which has the collective strength to help lift the nation out of recession. We've also made a deep dent in the unemployment rate—something that the politicians have yet to understand.

1

THE LONE RANGERS RIDE AGAIN

People, it seems, have once again disregarded expert prediction.

...what most astonished me in the United States is not so much the marvelous grandeur of some undertakings as the innumerable multitude of small ones.

—Alexis de Tocqueville, *Democracy in America*

Something quite dramatic is taking place.

It has attracted no headlines and tends to get most of its recognition in footnotes in Labor Department and Census Bureau reports. It has garnered approximately one-thousandth of the attention paid to the final episode of M*A*S*H* and has had about half as much impact on the general public consciousness as the advent of designer chocolates.

Yet it is a thing of great consequence. The old dream of self-employment is staging a major comeback after a full century of decline. Millions more Americans are their own bosses today than a decade ago and there is every reason to believe that the ranks of the self-employed will continue to swell as the 20th century winds down.

Ironically, this shift has been taking place during a time when the self-employed American appeared to be headed onto the endangered species list and then to full extinction. The experts were in near total agreement on this point.

THE SHRINKING WORLD

There was a time when the self-employed were in the clear majority, but by the time the distinction between self-employed and employed

was first tabulated in the 1870 Census, about a third of the workforce
was self-employed. In his studies of American workers, economist
Willford I. King charted these changes:

1870 = 34.1% self-employed
1880 = 32.2%
1890 = 30.4%
1900 = 30.0%
1910 = 24.9%

The trend was clear and continuing. Of course, as the population at
large grew so did the number of self-employed, but their proportion of
the population was declining. There were, for example, 4 million
more self-employed in 1930 than in 1880, but their overall percentage
had dropped 17% in the same period. Then, starting about 1940, the
numbers began to go down along with the percentages. Ironically, it was
at about this time that the term "self-employed" showed up in Paul C.
Berg's *Dictionary of New Words in English* as a neologism of the
1940s—as if created to describe something on the wane, an oddity.

By 1950, the percentage of the self-employed in the labor force had
gone up to 19.5%, but by 1960 it had dropped to 13.0% and in 1970 it
was down to 7%. With the notable exception of the construction field,
which has been a stronghold for self-employment, many professions
which had been most closely associated with autonomy and self-
employment seemed to be jumping on the organizational bandwagon.
The number of self-employed Americans in agriculture showed the
most dramatic decline both in percentage and in numbers, falling from
5.4 million in 1940 to 2.8 million in 1960.

By 1962, when Joseph D. Phillips published his study *The Self-
Employed in the United States*, there was ample proof to support a
common economic rule of thumb: the more developed an economy
the smaller will be the proportion of self-employed workers in its labor
force. Phillips cited examples of this from all over the developed
world: Canadian self-employment had dropped from 26% in 1931 to
15% in 1958,. Swiss self-employment had dropped from 30% in 1888
to 19% in 1950, Australian self-employment went from 21% in 1933
to 18% in 1954 and so forth. Needless to say, economists pointed to
the decline in American self-employment as a barometer signaling an
ever more sophisticated and developed economy.

In the late 1960s and early 1970s the picture seemed particularly
bleak. Government figures and projections on the number of self-
employed in the workforce continued to decline and we kept hearing
about the troubled and dying institutional havens for the self-
employed. By 1971 the Department of Labor was able to report that

the nation was securely employed by others, with a scant 6.7% of the workforce working for themselves. Fields in which workers were traditionally self-employed had been transformed as the 1971 statistics told us that most writers (62%) and most photographers (66%) were then being bossed by others.

AMERICA THE CORPORATE

A Social Security Administration study of the self-employed workforce from 1956 to 1970 concluded, "Growth of corporations, consolidation of farms, and low earnings in agriculture have gradually reduced the importance of self-employment as a component of the US Labor Force."

Meanwhile, large institutions seemed to be gorging themselves on new employees. During the 1960s the proportion of government employees went from 12% of the labor force to a full 15%. Out of the more than 3 million industrial units which employed 70% of the labor force in 1970, a mere 2% of those units employed more than half of those workers. The only major academic study of the self-employed, Phillips' *The Self-Employed in the United States*, looked at the causes for the decline and concluded, "The reasons for the decline of self-employment are many. No doubt the most important factor is the advantage of large-scale organization."

One clear advantage was the liberal collection of benefits that were offered to corporate employees. At the 1959 annual meeting of the General Electric Corp., its president, Robert Paxton, pointedly observed:

> The imposing list of benefits I cited does not adequately express the high level of benefits your company's employees enjoy. The value of our benefits is illustrated by the fact that a self-employed man aged 40 and earning $115 a week would have to increase his total weekly earnings by 35 percent in order to provide himself with take-home pay and benefits equivalent to those your company makes available to an employee of the same age and income. In fact, just two items on the list, insurance and pensions, would cost the self-employed man $1,061 annually, compared with $90 a year the General Electric employee pays directly as an addition to the payroll expense the company devotes to these two benefits.

Phillips also discovered something highly significant: that the self-employed in the age of *The Organization Man* and *The Man in the Gray Flannel Suit* tended to be the leftovers and corporate untouchables of the postwar boom. As he put it, "All in all, the world of the self-employed delineated by the statistical data is not primarily one of enterprise and independence, although these qualities are still found there. Rather, it is increasingly inhabited by older persons cut off from the main stream and by others lacking qualifications considered desirable by corporate employers. To some extent it is a refuge for the physically handicapped. Above all it is a shrinking world in a growing economy."

As the herds grew, it was hard to pick up the paper without reading about the demise of "mom and pop" grocery stores, one-lawyer law firms, family farms and the non-chain drug and hardware stores, among others. All sorts of forces seemed to be conspiring to drive the numbers down, ranging from the changing nature of agriculture to the expansion of the highway system, which was seen as an aid to large retailers and a detriment to local self-employed tradespeople.

The future looked even bleaker: a 1969 study from the Institute for the Future proclaimed that the self-employed American would virtually disappear from the scene by 1985 and Labor Department literature discussed self-employment as an element of the American workforce which was fast becoming more of a curiosity than an important factor. Phillips looked at the decline and predicted, "This trend will no doubt persist in the future."

Just to make sure the point wasn't lost, the Institute for the Future, among others, referred to the dying species as "lone rangers." It was therefore not surprising then that guidance counselors warned those entering the workforce to be wary of a self-employed future. The conventional wisdom was to say that the age of the independent entrepreneur was over and the future belonged to the acquisition-hungry conglomerates and ever growing government agencies.

THE WELL-KEPT SECRET

The warning was repeated in different ways but none was more dramatic than the 1973 release of the study *Work in America* by the Department of Health, Education and Welfare. This was the study commissioned by then-HEW Secretary Elliot Richardson which was noted for its unflinching condemnation of dull, repetitive, soulless work and its call for massive job redesign. One of the key findings of the study was that the problem in part stemmed from the growth of the large organization and bureaucracy and the diminishing opportunities to be one's own boss. Speaking of the opportunity to become self-employed, it said, "This element of the American Dream is rapidly becoming myth, and disappearing with it is the possibility of realizing the character traits of independence and autonomy..."

It viewed our society as one in which independence was venerated in the abstract but ignored in the concrete. For instance, the study pointed out, we were not giving our young people the knowledge they needed to go into business for themselves. "In fact," it added, "this knowledge is usually transmitted from father to son in middle-class families, and is thus difficult for women or the poor to obtain. Except for those young Americans who take part in Junior Achievement, knowledge about self-employment in this country is quite a well-kept secret." Dramatically, the report contrasted the virtues of self-employed autonomy and independence to the growing "tyranny of the bureaucracy" and increasing worker alienation at all levels. Its summation of the problem had a nearly apocalyptic ring to it: "It seems fair to conclude that the combination of the changing social character of American workers, declining opportunities to establish independence through self-employment, and an anachronistic organization of work can create an explosive and pathogenic mix."

For many of us who were then self-employed *Work in America* seemed to be the funeral oration for our form of work, and its depressing message was that the future belonged to the bossed and the herded. If we hung on, it seemed, it would indeed be as crusty, aging Lone Rangers riding off toward the 21st century.

The only optimistic thing about the report was that it brought up the possibility that the United States might consider encouraging certain types of self-employment through tax breaks, educational change, deregulation, reduced paperwork and new sources of risk capital. But this was one of a number of possible strategies outlined in the report, and it seemed like the type of notion that reports often tack on as something "to be explored."

What happened next was complex but simply explained: people did not behave in accordance with the statistics and forecasts and the well-kept secret was becoming common knowledge. The conventional wisdom of post-World War II America that we were all moving inexorably into work for big business, big labor and big government was wrong. It happened without the broad Federal reform and deregulation suggested in *Work in America*, which was, in the final analysis, well read and widely quoted but which raised more hackles than serious questions in the Nixon White House.

The Institute for the Future and the *Work in America* Task Force were not the only think tanks and august bodies to make a bad call on this point. Another band of futurists stressed an inner change in the nature of the population rather than the growing power of institutions as the reason for the decline in self-employment. In the 1960s the Stanford Research Institute produced a major report entitled *The World of 1975* which predicted a drift to a society in which security would become a *universal concern* among Americans "who will try harder than ever to insulate themselves from 'the slings and arrows of outrageous fortune.'"

The SRI study went on to say that the quest for security at work "will leave people somewhat empty, achievement satisfactions will be sought elsewhere. To relieve the feeling of guilt engennered by this, people will have a strong need to produce something tangible, something real and excellent. They will want to excel to fulfill the basic need for achievement."

To the SRI futurists the urge to excel would be fulfilled in education and leisure: "...whether the accent falls on the hobbyist making jewelry, the home mechanist at his lathe, the fisherman with superior tackle, or the reader buying handsome volumes for the pleasure they give."

Ironically, as it turned out, it was that very period around the "world of 1975" that the urge to become self-employed and reject the traditional notion of security in favor of risk rose at its most dramatic rate. Between 1972 and 1979 the number of self-employed rose by more than 1.1 million and the years 1976 to 1979 witnessed the first period in modern history when, according to the Bureau of Labor Statistics, the growth rate for the number of self-employed workers surpassed the comparable increase for wage and salary workers (12.4% for self-employed vs. 10.8% for the employed).

There had been what futurist John Naisbitt would term in 1981 a restructuring of society and an "explosion of entrepreneurial activity." Not only were the self-employment figures up, but so were the number of new business incorporations—topping 400,000 in 1977, going over 500,000 in 1979 and hitting 600,000 in 1983. There were many failures as well, but the fact remained that the urge to start was getting stronger.

Going back to the SRI report, it would seem that the hobbyist making jewelry went into the jewelry business and the fisherman with superior tackle went into the fly-tying business. What's more, antique lovers opened shops, good cooks began to dabble in professional catering and journalists went off to write the great American novel or, more realistically, start a specialized newsletter catering to a specific interest. Nor were all of these people going off to work that was chic and would keep their fingernails clean. Some were actually going off to do old-fashioned work: plating, plumbing, repairing and a hundred other things.

In fact, what happened closely paralleled the situation in rural America. At the precise time when it seemed that rural America was heading into a fatal tailspin—termed "the rural crisis" not so long ago—demographers were astonished to find a net gain of a million new rural residents. The key indicator of declining population had entirely turned around. The 1980 Census confirmed this and showed that between 1970 and 1980 the population of rural areas had grown at the same rate as that of urban areas. In fact the increased population of some rural areas was such that they had to be reclassified as urban.

With this came a return of small-scale farming for the first time since the family farm went into a tailspin after World War II. Government figures in the early 80s showed that close to half of the 2.8 million U.S. farms were less than 100 acres in size. Between 1980 and 1984 the number of farms with less than 50 acres jumped by 17% to 637,000 as the number of larger family farms declined. Many of these were owned by a new breed of farmer selling fresh produce directly to the consumer at farmer's markets, co-ops and roadside stands. The farmers found a market for the kind of tomatoes that you can't get in the supermarket, gourmet apples and straight-from-the-farm yogurt. They tended to read *Farmstead Magazine, Mother Earth News* and *Blair and Ketchum's Country Journal.* They were deemed by the *Washington Post* to be the "new phenomenon in farming, American style."

OUTSIDE INTERESTS

A major reason why people defied the self-employment forecasts was that large numbers of Americans found goals which lay outside large institutions. The perks, pension plans and promises of job security did not turn us all into organization men and women. Many people began to think about security in a new light in an era of conglomerates, mergers and "bottom line" management. Some things changed, but not the right of an employer to fire, lay off and close whole divisions. By the early 1980s even the concept of security in Federal government employment had been badly shaken as "bulletproof" jobs were shot full of holes by the Reagan Administration. Middle managers were being squeezed out of their jobs as corporations went on diets to become "leaner." After looking at a number of recent surveys, *Industry Week* magazine concluded in 1983 that a "middle-management malaise" pervaded American industry. A 1982 study by the Opinion Research Corp. concluded that worker satisfaction was at its lowest level since 1950.

The other side of the coin was that corporations and government agencies increasingly saw the logic of hiring independent contractors to perform specialized tasks. It was often cheaper and more efficient to contract with an outsider than hire someone. Bruce Phillips, an economist with the Small Business Administration, points out, "We see this trend in many sectors of the economy. If companies have come out of the last recession 'lean and mean' it is in part true because they have learned how to use independent workers." Another factor was the growth of smaller service and high-tech companies which use many self-employed. *Venture* magazine in a special report on self-employment stated, "The small firms need specialized help badly, but can't always afford to keep a stable of skilled technicians. Thus, a tremendous demand has arisen for consultants in a wide variety of fields, from engineering to finance." Others viewed the self-employed independent contractors as "buffers" against layoffs and firing—people who could be hired for a project with a clearly established beginning, middle and end.

The result was that self-employment, which was a persistent dream of the 1970s, was becoming one of the nicer realities of the 1980s. The same look of those outside in the 1950s, the wistful envy directed through the windows at the professionals in the offices, could now be seen on the faces of those inside, staring toward the seaside loft where sails are rigged, the artist's garret, bed and breakfast hostelries, the neighborhood wine and cheese shop or the one-person think tank where great new pieces of computer software would be created.

People acted on what they had known all along. In an era of mass production and giant corporations, self-employment allowed the individual to acquire immediate "hands-on" experience in his own field, instead of being swamped with isolated details, exposed only to the parts and never the whole. And for many people, one vital consideration was the opportunity to have control over the quality of the work, with no quotas or arbitrary deadlines to meet, no compromises required because of the meshing of input from other workers and departments. You are, in effect, your own quality control board and responsibility is considerable. If your "consumers" are dissatisfied with the quality of work, your business will fail.

One of the greatest specific forces at work was freedom itself, something that had been underestimated in the days when it was assumed that virtually all of us would rather have had a corporate dental plan or a parking spot with our name on it than a life infused with a whole new dimension of freedom. Much evidence supports this but nothing quite so graphically as a 1984 study which examined the motivation of 203 people who started their own businesses. The study, by the Comprehensive Accounting Corp., found that freedom was the strongest force at work and making more money was the second most important factor—by no means an insignificant factor in all of this.

For some there was the additional lure of working at home. Bringing the workplace back into the home opened up the possibility of a more fully integrated lifestyle, incorporating work, family and community. The home became, as it was in pre-industrial days, the focus of life and the worker became more concerned and involved with community interests, the neighbors and the day-to-day life of family members. All of this could have a long-term positive impact on society—greater community stability, for instance, and decreased alienation and disintegration within the family unit.

With this came a change in attitude and the small family business gained a new glamour. Sylvia Porter pointed out in a July 1984 column that it was not too long ago when the point of a family business was to work hard so that the next generation would receive the education needed to become executives or professionals. "For a son or daughter to move back to the family company meant either he or she couldn't cut it in the corporate world or had just flunked out of graduate school." Now, she said, there is new pride in the "businesses that have caused the family to prosper over the decades."

By 1983 the statistics put the self-employment turnaround into a realistic context as the Census Bureau was able to report that more than 2 million Americans were working in home-based businesses. To others this total was off the mark by millions. *Newsweek* pegged the total at 5 million and, according to the *Wall Street Journal*, a study by AT&T concluded that 7% of the working population was working at home full time and 6% had second jobs at home. With a workforce of 103 million, the AT&T study suggested more than 13 million full-and part-time at-home jobs.

It flew in the face of the way things had been planned and zoned. Work was supposed to be done downtown, in industrial parks and commercial strips, and a great body of regulations had been enacted to keep residential areas apart from business and commerce. The plan worked well for a long time but then the 20th century caught up with the division. Women went back to work, so that two parents were commuting downtown instead of just one.

The time, money and energy that went into getting to and from work doubled and the fast-food restaurants benefited as two people got home too tired to cook. School children came home to empty homes, and communities set up "latch-key hotlines" for kids to call when they were lonely or scared or in a jam. Some parents bought the kids computers and VCRs to amuse them—some started to figure out a way to work at home.

Another discovery—a major one: some found that they liked risk—actually craved a situation where success, failure and points in between were in their own hands. Stress be damned they said as they turned the knots in their stomachs into an asset. Risk was seen as the antidote to the white-collar blahs and the blue-collar blues or, as *Esquire* magazine publisher Phillip Moffitt put it in an editorial in his magazine, "Risk-taking is the mind's fuel; it stimulates the adrenaline, and while it may arouse much self-doubt and may cause sinking sensations in the stomach and gnashing of the teeth, it does not allow you to be bored."

And it was more than just a theory. In the survey of 1,500 Americans which Daniel Yankelovich conducted for his book *New Rules*, he found that nearly three out of four felt they had greater freedom of choice in how they lived their lives than their parents did. From this he traced a great willingness to take risks in all aspects of life including work.

To be sure there can be risk in employed work, but it is usually only alloted to those at the top—to those who have their own executive rest room keys—rationed like a rare brandy.

SUBCULTURAL REVOLUTION

The dream of self-employment has been a well-nourished one. "Own Your Own Business" shows and franchise expositions became popular, financial institutions advertised their desire to help the self-employed set up special Keogh retirement plans and we kept hearing those stories about people who walked away from successful jobs and headed off into a new independent direction...high-powered sales reps now running barbecue joints, the *Fortune* 500 executives rehabilitating and operating country inns, housewives building small catering empires and aerospace engineers recycling themselves as freelance toy designers. If you listened carefully, you began to get the notion that every third college graduate had decided to become a chimneysweep, blacksmith, organic farmer or freelance photographer.

As the aspiration to break away from employment to self-employment grew, the book publishers saw what was happening and brought us such works as *Money in Your Mailbox, Free Yourself in a Business of Your Own, How to Earn over $50,000 a Year at Home, 132 Ways to Earn a Living Without Working (For Someone Else), 1001 Ways to be Your Own Boss* and *Candlemaking for Profit*. Scores of these books were published in the mid through late 1970s and into the 80s, with some achieving a remarkable level of specificity, such as one revealing 31 self-employed pursuits to engage in while traveling around the United States in an RV.

Such was the new mood that anything seemed possible. A shelf-full of books came along listing the endless possibilities for independence. Some of these books trafficked in the oddest assortment of independent incarnations suggesting that such occupations as rabbit farmer, pet photographer and sexual surrogate could really support more than a handful of legitimate new operators. One book, Kathy Matthews' *On Your Own*, listed among its "99 Alternates to a 9 to 5 job" these fine vocations: collecting fireflies, detasseling hybrid corn, movie extra, selling mistletoe, sperm-bank contributor and fingernail farming (for anyone not familiar with this branch of agriculture, it refers to growing long nails, clipping them and selling them to beauty shops where they are transplanted onto other hands). This book also approaches some of the sleazier professions with disarming naivete. Under the heading of "exotic dancer" we are told, "The pay is better than average—often around $5 an hour for a beginner—and you can sometimes earn tips." It never mentions what exotic dancers do to get tips—gyrate lewdly in the nude—but it breathlessly informs us that many ballet dancers work part time as exotic dancers.

As if to underscore a point made by *Washington Post* writer Curt Suplee who said of self-help books, "There's a succor born every minute," you could get a copy of *Sunken Golf-Ball Recovery* for a mere $34.50 and *Yogurt Bar* for just a little bit more. Another book devoted a whole chapter to "Selling Nature Without Harming It," outlining the opportunities in such areas as the collection and sale of driftwood and supplying insects for serum production.

More often than not the books traded in big dreams as, for instance, more than one retold the story of Margaret Rudkin turning a home bakery into Pepperidge Farm. But this was as it should be—people do not take risks in order to fail.

Still others reveled in the "less is more" philosophy of it all and talked of it all in terms of meaningful lifestyles, human potential and self-sufficiency. Such books as John Applegath's *Working Free*, Geof Hewitt's *Working for Yourself* and Michael Phillips and Salli Raspberry's *Honest Business* stressed the idealism of self-employment and entrepreneurship. These books were clearly written for people who were more at home with *The Whole Earth Catalog* and the works of E. F. Schumacher than books with titles promising one's first million and the works of Dale Carnegie.

Clearly, attitudes were changing. Writing in *Working Woman* magazine, David E. Gumpert of the *Harvard Business Review* said, "Socially, entrepreneurship has become more acceptable than at any time in years—especially compared with the late 1960s and early 1970s, when it was in vogue to be anti-business." All of this was driven home most graphically in 1980 when former Yippie Jerry Rubin wrote in the *New York Times*, "The challenge for American capitalism in the 80s is to bring the entrepreneurial spirit back to America...America needs a revitalization of the small-business spirit."

BOX SCORE

While it took a while for the newly independent to show up in the official statistics, now they have and the results are continually impressive. There are a number of indicators now available and all of them are solidly positive. In no special order, we now know that:

- In August 1984, the last month for which there were complete statistics, there were 9.58 million self-employed in the United States based on figures from the Bureau of Labor Statistics.

This figure and almost all others on self-employment are deceptively low because of the fact that people who incorporate as individuals are not counted but considered to be employees of their own corporation. These private or professional one-person corporations are in reality self-employed but technically corporations. The last time they were tabulated was in 1979 when there were 2.1 million of them (up 40% from 1.5 million in 1976), and it is safe to presume that there are as many today and perhaps as many as a million more. Keeping this "incorporation factor" in mind dramatizes all of the statistics on the self-employed.

- Between 1975 and 1983 self-employment increased about 2 to 3% annually, approximately 200,000 individuals per year. This trend accelerated in the early 1980s and the number shot up by 497,000 between 1982 and 1983 and close to that amount between 1983 and 1984. The increase was summed up in a July 1984 article in the *Monthly Labor Review* by economist Eugene H. Becker: "...self-employment among American workers has been increasing for almost a decade and a half, barely pausing for cyclical downturns."
- Between 1972 and 1981 the percentage of American workers who were self-employed grew by 32%. Between 1978 and 1980, for the first time in modern American history, the rate of growth for the self-employed exceeded that for wage and salary workers.
- Although the number of non-white self-employed is small in absolute terms, it is growing at a faster rate than the population at large—45% during the same 1972 to 1981 period.
- During the same 1972 to 1981 period the female share of self-employment rose dramatically from 1,372,000 to 2,192,000 representing an absolute increase of 60%. Looking at it from still another statistical point of view, the female share of self-employed jobs was 26% in 1972 and 31% in 1981.

Beyond the raw statistics, certain interesting trends could be spotted. The Small Business Administration, in its 1983 *State of Small Business* report, saw some reasons for the rise. One of these, to quote the report, was: "In tight labor markets people turn to self-employment in order to start new businesses. For example, from 1974 to 1976, encompassing the 1974-1975 recession, the percentage of self-employed persons increased in thirty-four states." It is now clear that this was also true during the 1980-82 recession.

Secondly, said the report, "There appears to be a deeper structural change occurring in the economy which may lead to self-employment. A detailed study of the industrial economy of the industrial states might show that declines from 1970 to 1980 in durable good industries (e.g., in steel, autos, etc.) have been offset by extensive growth of the self-employed."

In all, there were 14 states and the District of Columbia in which the self-employed population grew faster than the number of wage and salary workers during the 1970s. Looking at the list, the Small Business Administration saw the old industrial states and the high-growth New England and Western states as the beneficiaries. These were the major hotbeds: Alaska, California, Connecticut, District of Columbia, Hawaii, Maine, Massachusetts, New Hampshire, New Jersey, New York, Pennsylvania and Rhode Island. Of these the leader was Alaska, with an overall rise of 7.7%. Only four states actually saw a decline in the percentage of the self-employed—Mississippi, North and South Dakota and North Carolina.

TURNING POINTS

If there was a historic moment when it was finally clear that the trend had reversed and could be proven with hard facts, it was in November 1980 when the Department of Labor issued a press release which opened, "The number of self-employed Americans is increasing dramatically, reversing decades of steady decline..."

There was an even more important moment in early 1984 when the Small Business Administration looked at the figures from the 1980-82 recession and the ensuing recovery and concluded, "Self-employed workers, who comprised only 7.6 percent of the civilian work force in 1983, have made a disproportionate contribution to the recent economic recovery."

This statement, which appeared in the 1984 *State of Small Business* report, amounted to official recognition of the fact that self-employment had become a force in the U.S. economy with the power to help get the nation out of recession.

No matter how you looked at it, the statistical evidence was clear and dramatic. Between the end of 1982 and the end of 1983 close to half a million new self-employed came along—this constituted a 6.6% rise compared to a 3.7% rise in wage and salary workers during the same period. During the 1980-82 recession there had been a small loss of wage and salaried jobs, but there had been a corresponding rise of 4.3% in non-farm self-employment. At the same time there was a drop-off in jobs with companies employing more than 500 people.

Looking at these facts and figures on the eve of their release in February 1984, SBA economist Bruce Phillips said, "We're watching a major change here. The love affair with large corporations is ending and people are looking for more flexibility. People seem to be trusting corporations less and themselves more. Certain kinds of business are easier to start and require brains but little capital. After all you can write a best-selling computer program on the bus."

Phillips was also aware of regional factors. He noted for instance that in the 1980-82 recession there were states in which self-employment had grown at a healthy rate in the face of a loss of wage and salary employment. "In Indiana, for instance, there was a four percent rise in non-farm self-employment but a loss of more than five percent of wage and salary jobs." He also noted that in some states self-employment income had significantly raised the overall level of income.

The situation in Canada is much the same. Not only has the self-employed population been increasing, but it has been growing at a rate faster than that of the number of paid workers.

In 1984 1,480,000 Canadians—or one of eight workers—were self-employed. These numbers contain 439,000 self-employed individuals who were incorporated. In a paper on self-employment in Canada published in the February 1985 issue of *The Labour Force*, Ian Macredie, director of the Economic Characteristics Division of Statistics Canada, wrote of the growth period from 1979 to 1984: "Perhaps the most significant difference is found in the changes from 1981 to 1982 [during the recession] where paid worker employment declined by 375,000 (-3.9%) while self-employment actually increased by 27,000 (+2.0%). The higher growth rate in self-employment continued in the post-recession recovery period with the number of self-employed persons increasing by 61,000 (+4.4%) from 1982 to 1983, compared to 32,000 (+0.3%) for paid workers."

During the same 1979-84 period, Macredie also found that the proportion of self-employed workers increased from 12.0% to 13.5% of the total number of employed. Another Statistics Canada analyst, Jean-Marc Levesque, published a companion paper in which he took a close look at the effect of recession on self-employment and found that while some of the growth came from laid-off workers, "much of the increase occurred in the service sector, where the unemployment rate was relatively low; this suggests that the rate of increase in the number of self-employed workers was only partially affected by the economic conditions prevalent in the labour market at the time."

Meanwhile, the prospects for self-employment in the late 1980s and 1990s look even brighter as a diverse set of factors bid to have continued impact.

One of the most significant of these factors has been the emergence of the entrepreneurial woman. This has been happening for a number of reasons: the desire to start work on one's own terms outside a traditional hierarchy, the desire to work at home and the desire to get out of a dead-end position in a large organization. Another point is made by David A. Hirschberg, an economist with the SBA's Office of Advocacy, who feels that there now may be a limit to the number of jobs which women will be able to find as they try to enter the workplace and more and more of them may choose to set up shop on their own. Hirschberg adds that this comes at a time when barriers—such as the difficulty in getting credit—are disappearing.

"Women," said Ronnie Feit, who directed the government's Interagency Committee on Women's Business Enterprise, "are now in the role of outsider coming into the marketplace—our new immigrants. Historically, outsiders have tried to enter on their own terms and this means as your own boss." This point has not been lost on those who would like to supply the woman in business. "There's one place where women get a fair shake—that's when they're in business for themselves," says radio personality Paul Harvey in a Servicemaster radio ad.

The emergence of the entrepreneurial woman appears to be occurring throughout the industrialized world. In some places the results are quite dramatic. In Sweden the number of women entrepreneurs increased by 11,700 between 1972 and 1982 while the number of men in business for themselves dropped by 3,900 during the same period. In the United States all the barometers point to the conclusion that women are becoming independent and entrepreneurial at a faster rate than men. The most telling statistic of all: in 1977 the Bureau of the Census found 702,000 women-owned businesses in the United States—in 1982 the Internal Revenue Service found 2.8 million.

Other encouraging considerations apply to both men and women. There has been some lessening of federally required paperwork and beginning in 1984 self-employed have had the right to set aside more Keogh pension money than ever before. Still another is the bandwagon effect which will take place as old conventions change: fathers and/or mothers passing along family businesses to daughters as well as sons, the growing acceptance of second careers as more than a mere curiosity and, simply, more people realizing that there is life beyond the large institution.

Another factor is a general one with specific attributes. The very things that once seemed to be the exclusive property of large organizations are now becoming available to the individual. In this regard, technology has been in the lead. Not too many years ago new technology was seen as a barrier to independence as one fretted about how to compete with an organization and all of its electronic gizmos. Today, telephone-answering machines, sophisticated calculators, photocopy machines and small computers are relatively cheap, plentiful and fit into the operation that "starts on a shoestring."

In addition, advances in computer technology have made it possible to do certain kinds of work at home which had previously required the presence of a large support staff and face-to-face dealings in offices or manufacturing plants. These new developments, say a number of people beginning with Alvin Toffler in *The Third Wave*, will eventually allow the de-centralization and de-urbanizatiin of production. A greater percentage of workers now deal with intangibles, "information," as opposed to "things" and could already be working at home.

Beyond technology per se are factors as diverse as the increased liberalization of tax write-offs for the technology and the banding together of self-employed people to obtain benefits ranging from mutual support to group rates for medical insurance. It is also becoming a political fact of life that hip-pocket trade associations composed of independent operators—ranging from flea market czars to pizza parlor dons—are beginning to learn how to lobby in their members' interests. Others are using networks which vary from quite informal to formal, featuring meetings, seminars and newsletters.

This kind of loose organization may be one of the key elements which has nurtured the new breed of self-employed American and which may make it easier for those now coming along. The idea is hardly new—granges, co-ops, guilds and the like have existed for years—but what is new is the proliferation of these groups and their spread into areas which have traditionally shunned organization altogether.

Writers are a case in point. A score or more regional and topic-oriented associations for freelance writers have come into being in recent years. Washington Independent Writers, a group with which the author is involved, got going in 1974 with initial hopes of attracting a hundred or so members in the Washington, D.C. area. It now boasts a membership of over 1,200 and offers those members benefits as diverse as a Job Bank, a director, a legal defense fund, a newsletter, medical and legal insurance plans, workshops and social events including an annual office Christmas party (for those who miss that ritual of the white-collar employed). This group and others like it are making it easier for independent writers to make a living.

Similarly, new services for the self-employed—often provided by other self-employed individuals—have become a growth industry in their own right. Outside answering and secretarial services, computer time-sharing companies, newsletter publishers, temporary rent-an-office agencies and specialized consultants are but a part of this service group.

Still another factor is one which lacks a generally recognized name but which can be typified by a growing flexibility and willingness to experiment. Many enter the ranks of the self-employed after first trying it out on a part-time basis while still holding a full-time job. Though there are no statistics on the trend it is widely believed that a large number of those coming into the field first learned about it and made contacts as part-timers. Then there is the growing awareness that family life can be beneficially rearranged around a self-employed career. Self-employed fathers who work at home, for instance, tend to become more involved in child rearing and the total household economy. Self-employed mothers, on the other hand, tend to have a great deal more flexibility in their lives than their regularly employed counterparts.

Some have tried to put a name on this new flexibility which goes beyond the issue of self-employment into a broader state of being. Tony Jones, a New York writer, in an article for *Creative Living* magazine called it "the New Autonomy," the crux of which is "the growing opportunity for people to shape their lives according to inner impulse or conviction." Jones adds, "It is as if significant numbers of people were suddenly free to think of themselves as artists with life as their canvas. And with this further option—if they do not like the picture at any point, they can step to a fresh easel and begin again from a new perspective."

OFF THE BOOKS

One factor—albeit a negative one—that cannot be overlooked is the *underground economy,* in which one earns money but doesn't pay income taxes or make Social Security payments. There has always been an underground economy, but as taxes have increased so too has the desire to avoid them. It is almost impossible to avoid taxes while working for a large organization, but not always that difficult if you are unobtrusively self-employed.

A major Internal Revenue Service study released in 1979 concluded that at least a billion dollars was being lost annually in taxes because of

independent contractors who either reported none of their income or
only part of it. The IRS zeroed-in on a sample of 7,000 individuals in
selected fields (real estate, trucking, logging, consulting, insurance,
franchise operations, construction and ten others) and discovered that
almost half of them (47%) reported *no income*. In some areas the
percentage of workers not reporting any income was remarkable, with
warehousing (80% not reporting), logging and timber (69.5%) and
taxicabs (64.7%) in the lead.

Predictably, perhaps, those making the least were the least likely to
report their income—67.2% of those with an adjusted gross income of
less than $5,000 admitted no income while 11.1% in the $100,000 and
over category did not report a penny of it. These disclosures had a
stunning initial effect on official Washington. At first, Congress
seemed to be moving toward a law which would make all those who
contract with independents withhold a percentage of their fees, but it
ended up doing little more than clamping down on waiters, waitresses
and others who depend on tips.

Some estimates have made the IRS calculation of a billion dollars
seem like small change. Edgar Feige, an economist at the University of
Wisconsin in Madison, pegs it at 30% of the GNP—an outlaw economy
of $700 billion, which is larger than France's GNP. Feige counts
everything in his estimate including flea market and garage sale
income. A more recent study by the Census Bureau for Congress
concluded that it is only about $222 billion.

There is a school of thought that uses the underground economy to
infer that there are many, many more self-employed people at work
than appear in the official statistics. If so, many of those now showing
up as unemployed should actually be listed as self-employed. In
Novembee 1979 Peter Gutmann, professor of economics at Baruch
College in New York City, created a stir when he told the Joint
Economic Committee of Congress that the official figures were missing
as many as 5 *million underground self-employed individuals*. Gutmann's
conclusion has been challenged but only in terms of the size of the
group. The 1983 study of the underground economy by the Census
Bureau pegged the full-time underground self-employed at 700,000
individuals (along with 1,800,000 wage and salary workers with an
underground occupation). Whatever its actual size nobody doubts that
a sizable group exists. It is also clear that another large segment of the
underground economy comprises self-employed "underreporters"
who fiddle with their bottom lines either by accepting money "off the
books" or by claiming illegal deductions. It was therefore not shocking
when an IRS spokesman said in 1983, "Self-employed individuals with
complicated tax returns are the most likely to be audited."

One of the more curious effects of the outlaw economy has been that it helps belie the notion that the Orwellian 1984 is upon us. Several of those who have rebutted it have pointed out that if there is a Big Brother he is one who cannot judge the size of the underground economy let alone control it.

URGENT BUSINESS

Finally, there is the factor of the urge itself. Self-employment as its own goal. The desire to manage one's own life, to become a whole unto oneself rather than be part of a larger whole and to take risk are all mixed together in an exciting package. People who have actually done it talk about it in terms of excitement, daring and boldness: terms which seem more appropriate to the athletic field than the workplace. These forthright words stand in direct contrast to the employed workplace where the flabby, bloated language of the behavioral sciences have long obtained. The self-employed worker can be happy, the employed worker can attain a high-level of self-actualization through job enrichment. The self-employed worker can be scared and unhappy, but his employed counterpart has to deal with dissatisfaction and alienation.

Yet the urge fits in with the vogue concepts of the day—local self-sufficiency, smallness, industrial democracy and what Alvin Toffler has lumped into his "Third Wave," which he describes as a new code of personalized schedules, lowered scale and heightened individuality.

In this popular Tofflerian scenario, work will increasingly take on a personal dimension. Life will no longer be so rigidly compartmentalized—the relationship between your "personal" life and your "career" will no longer be dictated by the opposite ends of a commuter route but will co-exist, interrelate and mutually influence one another.

The flexibility needed to blur the distinctions between home and work and work and play is not going to come from an employer whose strengths are based in management, control and a *workplace*. Such flexibility, however, exists from the very moment a person becomes self-employed.

The significance of time cannot be overstated in all of this as more and more people realize that it is more important than either power or money. John Applegath, author of *Working Free: Practical Alternatives to the 9-to-5 Job*, has termed having control over your own time "a potent new status symbol." A recent Department of Labor study would seem to confirm this: 48% of the people who were asked if they would rather have more money or more time said more time.

There are other reasons why the self-employment option is an important one to keep open. Ranging from its function as a damper to unemployment—turning a laid-off teacher into a self-employed tutor, for instance—to its use as a working alternative to the world of large organizations, it has great social value. For many the underlying motivation at work here is that even with definite drawbacks, self-employment is a far more satisfying and free form of work than can be found in most organizations and is especially appropriate for those who do not want or need supervision and cannot identify with hierarchies.

It also has other uses for society. For one, there is a great demand for part-time work in the United States. A 1981 Lou Harris poll showed that 28% of working men and 48% of working women would prefer to work part time. Another 1981 survey—taken among employees 55 years of age and older who were working for a major life insurance company—found that 85% were at a point in their lives at which they preferred to work part time. There are limits to the number of part-time jobs offered by corporations and government agencies, but there are no such policy limits on self-employment. Much the same can be said of second careers, for which there also seems to be considerable demand. The American Management Association found in a survey in the early 1970s that some 44% of middle managers envisioned themselves in a second career.

Finally self-employment is important for its influence on employment. Many of the changes which are taking place in the workplace are a clear attempt to give people some of the freedoms which accrue to the self-employed. These range from changes in customs which affect the scheduling of work (shared jobs, flexitime and so forth) to changes in the job itself which give the worker more freedom and autonomy.

THE IMPOSSIBLE DREAM

Self-employment also functions as a daydream. As most self-employed people will report, they are constantly told by their employed friends and neighbors how they harbor the notion of striking out on their own. For the dreamers, this will occur *someday*...when the moment is right...when the kids have finished school...when I get a few extra bucks put away...when I come up with the right idea...when I simply can't take another day at work. Others are ultimately weighted down by their liberal benefit packages. They can dream but really can't imagine walking away from the pension plan, the stock options, the paid vacations and sick leaves.

Those who have studied comparative forms of work have come to the strongest support of self-employment. In *Where Have All The Robots Gone?* a large-scale study of worker dissatisfaction in the 1970s, it was concluded, "Work dissatisfaction, life dissatisfaction were practically nonexistent among the self-employed," and the Department of Health, Education and Welfare's influential *Work in America* study not only described it as "the most satisfying of all kinds of employment" but called for new mechanisms to make employed work more like self-employed work.

All of this is not to say that the picture is uniformly bright. Some professional areas of traditional self-employment have become inhospitable to independents. For instance, one of our most cherished American credos is the belief in the independent inventor tinkering his or her way to the next Xerox machine or Polaroid camera. Yet that revered tradition of Edison, Bell and the Wright brothers has been severely weakened—just one of a number of weakened independent traditions.

Beginning immediately after World War II, the independent self-employed inventor began to go into eclipse from a long-established dominant position. By 1950 only 45% of all patents were being granted to independents, with the rest going to companies, foundations, universities and government agencies. Today the individual share hovers around 22% to 24% of the total. Meanwhile, many, if not most, of today's individual inventors hold regular jobs, which means that the number of full-time inventors is quite small.

The reasons for this turn of events are several. For one, the cost and red tape associated with getting a patent have increased to the point where just getting the patent requires a minimum of a thousand dollars in registry and attorney fees and may cost many times that in the case of a sophisticated invention. Recently an official of the Small Business Administration estimated that it takes an average of $5,000 to obtain a patent and $250,000 to defend it if it is challenged. Another factor which has worked against the lone inventor is the great emphasis placed on large-scale innovation through massive government research and development programs.

However, despite the rising odds against independent inventors, they did not go away. In fact, there has recently been a small increase in the actual percentage of individuals getting patents as opposed to the 1970s. There has also been a real growth in inventors' groups, which collectively push the idea of individual, grassroots inventors. One estimate is that there are between 50 and 100 of these groups, many of which have sprung up in the last few years. There is even a newly formed National Congress of Inventor Organizations which acts as an umbrella organization for the others. The optimism and determination which have fueled this banding together must be looked on as a bright sign. Clearly there is also considerable inspiration in the fact that much of the computer software boom is a product of cottage industry.

SUBSPECIES

"Self-employed" is a term that is sometimes misused to describe the classic small business entrepreneurs who raise venture capital and manage employees. The true self-employed usually start alone or as mom and pop operations and stay that way—some become classic small businesses. The term does describe a wide range of activities and a motley occupational assortment ranging from street vendors to brain surgeons.

For this reason, the species begs to be broken down into subspecies:

Traditionalists

Those who have purposefully opted for independence in their work and life in traditionally self-employed professions—doctors, lawyers, small business owners, carpenters, architects, funeral directors and too many others to mention. Generally, these are people whose self-employment is a given and, barring a calamitous bankruptcy, who go through their working life without working for a salary.

Marginalists

Those who are self-employed because there is little else available to them—street vendors, migrant farm workers and women who take in other people's laundry, for instance. As this second category of workers represents mostly those who have accepted "marginal self-employment" as a matter of survival, the fact that it is tending to get smaller (though swelling during recession) is fortunate.

Recyclists

Those who make abrupt changes in their life, benefit and security patterns to fulfill independent goals ranging from corporate public relations experts who go off to work on their novels to couples in their 40s who have decided they would rather run a rural mom and pop antique shop than spend the rest of their working lives commuting to corporate jobs.

Some of the people within this group become self-employed to fulfill a specific working goal (running a country inn, starting a newsletter, novel or whatever) while others look at self-employment as an end in itself and would probably be just as happy with any one of a dozen self-employed careers. This latter group tends to be self-employed for the freedom and other ideological reasons.

Hybridists

People who are fully employed but moonlight in a self-employed occupation as well as those whose primary work is their own but take an employed second job. According to recent Labor Department statistics, some 34% of all American moonlighters are self-employed on their second job, but work for wages and salaries on their main job, while 7% of the nation's dual jobholders are primarily self-employed. As of May 1980, the most recent date for which figures are available, 1.9 million Americans fit into this "hybrid" category. There is reason to think that government figures in this area may be on the short side as it may be easier to hide one-half of your work if you are working at two different jobs, especially if one job has taxes automatically deducted and the second requires the individual to initiate the taxation. Wayne I. Boucher, Senior Researcher at the Center for Futures Research at the University of Southern California, has thought about those who are *both* self-employed and employed and said, "Since not everyone in this pool reports all earned income, this group may not only be the largest section of the underground economy, but also a significant savings source for venture capital in the country." Boucher notes that this group includes, but goes way beyond, traditional moonlighters. "In many instances," he says, "it is well nigh impossible for anyone but the person himself who is involved to tell when employment begins and self-employment ends."

Between these four groups there are great disparities in income and amenity levels. Many of the traditionalists make more than their salaried counterparts, but they are only part of the picture, as many of the self-employed cluster at the lowest economic level. A Census Bureau analysis of the situation in the early 1970s showed that while only 5% of the wage and salaried workers in the United States made less than $4,000 a year, 16% of the self-employed population were in that same bottom bracket.

While many of these low-income self-employed fall into the marginalist category, a number are also recyclists and hybridists "paying the price" of reduced income or longer hours in order to be their own boss, set their own rules and find satisfying work.

A case in point is freelance writing, which has long been a magnet for those who would like to escape the workaday world for "exciting" magazine assignments and "lucrative" book advances. Reality intrudes. PEN American Center, a New York-based writer's group, surveyed its members to see how they had fared financially in 1978. From 358 responses it was found that only 8% earned more than $50,000 but 9% earned nothing. A full 68% earned less than $10,000 from their writing and the median for the group was $4,700. One member, however, did make $800,000. A later and much larger survey was released by the Columbia University Center for the Social Sciences in 1981. Its survey of 2,239 book writers found that the average person was making only $4,775 a year from writing and that almost half of the nation's professional writers had paid jobs in addition to working on their writing. Only the top 10% was making over $45,000 a year and one had to get into the top 5% to find incomes over $80,000.

Although there are many sacrifices involved, one that is less so than ever before is time. For years in order for the self-employed person to keep up with the salaried Joneses, he or she had to expect to work longer hours. Census Bureau research told the story. Men who worked for themselves earned about as much as their salaried counterparts on the average, but put in much longer hours—51.5 hours per week as contrasted with 42.4 employed hours. Self-employed women, on the other hand, tended to earn less than their employed sisters. Recent statistics, however, show that the averages for self-employed men and women are going down and in 1983 for the first time the Bureau of Labor Statistics reported that the average American self-employed worker worked 40.0 hours a week.

BENES FROM HEAVEN

If there is a real sacrifice, it comes in the area of "employee benefits."

The employee benefit package has become a major financial factor separating the employed from the self-employed. If the urge to become one's own boss has increased, benefits for the employed have grown as well. These benefits may not be deterrents to making the decision to leave a job, but once the decision is made, the security gap suddenly widens frighteningly. People who break with organizations have to cope with *benefit shock.*

If there is a bright side to this, however, it is that the promise of ever greater perks and benefits for the employed has not quite lived up to expectations, and the Golden Age of benefits envisioned in the era of the Great Society has not panned out. In 1969 the Institute for the Future conducted a study which looked forward to major changes in employment and employee benefits in 1985. This was the same study which predicted that the employed American of the mid-1980s would have acquired a broadly expanded benefit package while the self-employed American would have become a bona fide rarity. One scenario of the world of 1985 went like this:

> Employee benefits have merged with compensation, social welfare, and on-the-job amenities; it is difficult to tell where one ends and the others begin. They are integrated in the minds of employers, employees, and the government. In effect, the environment created by the integration of social welfare programs and benefit programs required by legislation and existing as a result of agreements between labor and management has guaranteed all employees reasonable wages, more education and leisure, safer and more pleasant working places, and the avoidance of most of the fiscal hazards associated with accidents, ill health and old age. The programs mesh together: we have translated at least part of our capacity for economic production into *security*. The "rugged" individual who wants to take his wages in cash instead of guarantees against adversity has almost passed from the scene.

Beyond this general overview were the specific perks which were envisioned for 1985:

* Employers will pay about 50% of payroll in benefits.
* Benefits will generally reflect cost of living. For example, cost of living escalators will be built into most pension plans, effectively guaranteeing the pensioner a standard of living rather than a dollar amount.
* The 35-hour workweek and flexible working hours will be common, and more holidays and longer vacations will be the norm.
* Corporate-owned leisure facilities will be available to most employees, along with many more leisure-oriented benefits.
* It will be common to find on-site education programs and facilities, and some firms will provide educational leaves and even paid sabbaticals for employees.
* Subsidized housing and company cars will be available to many employees, along with savings plans in which the employer matches the employee's deposits.
* Expansive employee-counseling programs on matters as diverse as taxes, investments and retirement will be widespread.
* Psychiatric and dental care provisions will be part of the standard package of medical benefits.
* Since individual automobile insurance costs will have zoomed out of sight, group car insurance offered through the company will become the norm.
* Interconglomerate pension plans will have been established nationally, ushering in the day of the truly movable pension.

The Institute saw employed society moving in the direction of a world which had been described in a 1967 essay by Alvin Toffler, "The Concept of Post-economic Work," as one in which "want ads would seek employees on the basis of the kind of experience the employing company would supply. Instead of merely offering hospitalization, sabbaticals, and on-the-job training, the employer might offer the best educational facilities, the most progressive psychologists and the best sensory gratification chambers in the country."

Needless to say, a lot of this falls far short of the mark. Benefits run closer to 35% of the average American income (up from 23% in 1967) than 50% and, unless people are keeping it a secret, there are not too many group automobile insurance plans, 35-hour weeks or sensory gratification chambers in existence. In fact, the workweek is still very close to a standard 40 hours, which is exactly what it was at the end of World War II. Magazine and newspaper articles on the coming 35-hour workweek have been conspicuously missing of late. Meanwhile, inflation has made pensions seem a little less attractive, and in the popular mind, Social Security is a subject that creates more anxious feelings than secure ones. One recent survey indicated that as many as a third of recent retirees were forced into retirement by their employers.

The point, however, is that the lure of better and better benefit packages has become part of our expectations. If there is any consolation in all of this for the self-employed it is that a benefits Utopia is still not here.

LURID DETAILS

Benefit shock is, at best, a tough item with which to contend, but not as tough as it appeared to the experts back in 1969. The rugged loner in the study is a vital part of the present scene and shows no sign of passing.

In addition to benefit shock, there are a number of other drawbacks, cautions and problems ranging from the general loss of job security to specific roadblocks like neighborhoods where home-based business is in violation of local zoning laws. Other considerations: credit difficulties, erratic payment patterns, higher Social Security payments (for years the government has called this the self-employment tax) and the need to keep highly detailed financial records. Then there is the business of the many hats you will have to wear. While the self-employed are generally thought to be pursuing a specialty such as plastering or piano playing, most must devote great chunks of time to playing the many roles of an institution. Many find that besides their prime vocation they must also be their own promoter, sales rep, bill collector, accountant, treasurer, secretary, coffee shop, janitor, tax consultant and trash removal service. As much as we love the big picture, we must all become masters of piddling detail, carefully documenting the expenditure for every box of rubber bands and laboring over old phone bills to determine which calls were really for business. When we lunch together we split the check and fight over who gets the receipt and there is probably not one of us who at one time or another didn't end up going through the trash looking for an important sales slip. We wrap our own packages, sharpen our own pencils and run our own errands.

Yet even with all of the disadvantages lumped together, they add up to a respectable hurdle but hardly an insurmountable one.

The major advantages which define the aspiration to be self-employed—freedom, job ownership, happiness—are very real and more than offset the disadvantages. If the word *autonomy* ever seemed like an academic abstraction it becomes vivid reality—a glorious thing on the best of days; a ghastly burden on the worst of days.

Beyond the major considerations is still another lure of a new quality of life in which one's days change and take on an entirely new complexion. It sinks in that you really don't have to work on a given morning and this fact, oddly, impels you to work twice as hard. You learn to goof off with gusto, loudly proclaiming that the afternoon is your toy. Some aspects of these days are good, some bad—but almost all are of one's own doing and, as many who are self-employed will testify, become habit forming.

These new days are a mixture of many things...new and sometimes contradictory concepts of time ("When one is on one's own, is every day Saturday or Monday or is every day a little of each?")...the continuing realization that the term "striking out on one's own" has two meanings...discovering that paper clips are actually bought in stores and not "borrowed" from employers and that free photocopying is not a privilege handed down from the Magna Carta...becoming protective of your time, which is now truly your own time...and, if you work at home, blissfully and sadistically listening to morning and evening traffic reports on the radio—just as you imagine the President of the United States and other work-at-homes do.

Then there are the bona fide triumphs which mean so much to the self-employed: paying a bill on time, getting paid for your goods or services on time, getting paid (period), noting offhandedly that you might be able to make it for another year, and ending one project and launching another without getting ten administrators into the act.

Once such triumphs begin to occur with any frequency, the habit becomes hard to break. One concludes that despite the long-term trend and fat benefit packages of others, one has passed the point of no return. If outright financial disaster has been averted, the dreams of unbridled success continue. You keep running across those statistics on how the vast majority of new businesses fail in the first few years and, rightly and correctly, swear off statistics. You find yourself siding more and more with the underdogs of the world, tend to have new tolerance for the anachronistic and find that your intolerance for the blatantly bureaucratic has grown.

Paradoxically, it is hard to figure out where you fit into the scheme of things. Are you a pre-bureaucratic throwback having a momentary revival or the advance guard for the new era of fragmentation and working freedom?

"Is all of this just a new trap," you ask yourself, "with its own constraints, limitations and demands on freedom?" Perhaps so, but if it is, at least it is a trap of one's own design and, for that reason, a pretty good place to live and a great place to work.

Let us now move on to some old-fashioned personal testimonial—starting with the author's own bit of drumbeating. It will be upbeat drumbeating, but I have made sure to include a few honest, but sour notes as parts of the score.

2

TESTIMONIAL

Tales, Triumphs and Tribulations
Suggested by an Illegal Right Turn

About a year after I became self-employed I accidentally made an illegal right turn in my car and was issued a written warning by a policeman. At one point in the warning ritual he asked the name of my employer and I told him that I was self-employed. He shrugged and checked off the box on the form which said unemployed.

It was a warning in more than its intended sense because it served to graphically point out that I was a walking oddity in a world where normal people either had a job or were unemployed. It was the moment at which I really began thinking about being self-employed, thinking of myself as a full-fledged independent worker without an organization, stated policies or a regular paycheck. Somehow the enormity of my decision was brought home by the fact that for a fleeting moment at least, I was considered unemployed in the eyes of the law.

I long ago lost that sense of oddness—in fact, daily commuting and ritualistic staff meetings are what now seem odd—but since that day when I made the illegal turn there hasn't been a day in which I have not given some thought to the fact that I am self-employed. Most days I think of it favorably and I revel in the contrasts to the times when I worked for someone else or thought what it would be like if I had gone back to work in a corporation. Once in a while there is a bad day—one in which I roll the dice and land on the space that says go back five spaces—and I think that I am kidding myself and that it is all an illusion.

Over the years I can think back to many days in which the whole thing seemed to be backfiring and for every one of those days I can recall there are probably five that I've conveniently repressed. The one that most quickly comes to mind was not a day but three long weeks in which I struggled with a book idea that simply didn't work. On the Monday morning of what was to be the fourth week of the project I looked at what I had done and realized that it was going nowhere and that I had better cut my losses. And as hard as I looked at it, I found that I could salvage nothing. I couldn't blame anyone, bill anyone or find anything to write it off against—no brain depreciation allowance, an idea suggested by writer Larry King some years ago as a writer's answer to the oil depletion allowance. I hadn't even learned anything because the only lesson which had been underscored was one I already knew: that work can go up in smoke. Poof!

When I had a job as a writer for a company, work had gone up in smoke as well, but it was different because it was subsidized smoke for which I was paid a salary, and the expenses I incurred while producing that smoke wafted into the overhead where they were absorbed without notice. I even had an expense account which worked for both success and failure.

But everybody has bad days and although mine are unsubsidized, they are often of my own doing. Sometimes I get to save one on my own, usually helped by a bit of luck and the willingness to restart the day at 3:00 in the afternoon and defer Miller time to midnight. Once in a while, you make a save that is so nice and smooth that it is more satisfying than a day that worked well from the beginning.

UP FROM SALARY

Occasional bad days notwithstanding, it is clear to me that with each passing week the idea of working directly for someone else is no longer just a simple matter of taste or preference, but of something much deeper. The image that sticks with me is that of a domesticated animal which is let loose in the wilderness and becomes wilier and more self-sufficient by the day. Under the right pressure and with the right handler there is little question that the animal could be re-housebroken and lap trained, but it would not do so willingly.

So it is that I could go back to work if it were a matter of survival, but so many of the trappings and customs of institutional life now strike me as absurd. I think back to the long rambling meetings which went nowhere, the endless series of trivial memos, interminable chains of command, comically complex organizational charts, and official dictum and policy on matters ranging from promotions to parking spaces. For some reason to someone outside of an organization it is often policy—or preordained thinking—which seems most absurd because it is the term which institutions use to cover their most fossilized notions. These were all things which were part of my life when I was in my 20s, but now they seem like tribal rituals which I witnessed on some distant island when I was a young man and more tolerant of such things.

I have a lot of friends who live on the islands and I visit the islands from time to time in my work. The employed islanders love to ask self-employed people how they maintain the discipline needed to work where there are no bosses and no stated policy. The islanders always say that they would not have the discipline to work on their own. Yet it is the islanders who have to have extraordinary discipline. Daily commuting takes discipline, as does going to meetings and working on reports that nobody will ever read or working on something that everybody knows doesn't really need doing but which the boss wants done anyhow.

A lot of this fascinates me in the same way that an anthropologist becomes fascinated with the odd rituals and behavior patterns of some distant tribe. I love to hear people talk about how they have successfully plotted to get a day off without having it charged against their vacation time, or how the struggle has been won and they now have a corner office with a window. Some are little anthropological gems and are remembered for years:

- A Ph.D. scientist working until 3:00 A.M. on an experiment but still having to be in at 9:00 A.M. that same morning because his boss was nervous about having people absent who were not actually on vacation. This is the odd ritual of appearances which comes in many shapes and forms. In another version, people are expected to LOOK BUSY even when they're not.
- A Christmas party to which a man I know invited his friends as well as a group of the highest ranking executives in the company he worked for. Throughout the evening he referred to his friends by their first names and the others as Mr. and Mrs.
- A journalist tells me that the one disadvantage of his newly installed computer/word processing system is that the "people on the 12th floor" have so configured the system that they can electronically call up work in progress to see how people are doing. It drives him nuts. He thinks of it as the same as having someone looking over his shoulder at all times and he feels much more tentative about the way he writes. Now he is much less likely to try something daring or different because he fears it will be intercepted in the rough and he will look foolish. It is just one more example of an organization following its natural urge to insert that extra level of supervision which, as often as not, brings on a new level of inefficiency in the supervised.

I'm sure that somewhere there is a psychologist who, in this age of groups, teams and institutions, sees this as an abnormal fascination and that I am a certifiable institution-baiter and may even fit some of the less noxious characteristics of being anti-social. I'd plead guilty to all of this except for the anti-social part, which is altogether untrue. In fact, I have carefully worked to make sure that I have a lot of social contact during and after working hours and often wish I had more.

I do miss the comradeship of the watercooler and the chance to grab a quick, informal lunch with my co-workers. Looking back I realize that such meetings had great value and were, at once, a chance to test ideas, find out what was going on, gossip and have a few laughs. I don't miss this as much now because I'm at a point where I've replaced it with a group of a dozen or so other self-employed writers. We keep in contact by phone and dawdle over an occasional lunch or late afternoon beer. It takes work and time to keep in place but is very informal. In fact, it is so informal that I seldom think of it as anything more than having some good friends in the business who occasionally hang out together. The vogue term for this is networking, but that implies something more formal and dynamic, more like something that requires a diagram. To me it is a lot closer to the feeling of the watercooler than a network. Regardless of what I call it, it did take a long time for it to take shape and there were times when I felt terribly lonely for contact with others who were doing what I was doing.

SOLO TAKEOFF

But the truth is that when it comes to day-to-day work—that which we are doing at 9:15 on Monday morning—I'd much prefer to be on my own. Part of this is purely practical. If one figures that a person is given a limited amount of time to do what he's got to do, then there are cases where an institution is a hindrance. From the beginning of my self-employment I've been stunned to realize how much more there was to a day when it was stripped of its organizational fluff. For at least the first year of my liberation, there was not a day in which I did not actually revel in the fact that I had stepped into a realm where time had an extra dimension.

The fluff I was not free from came in many forms and from many sources, but the worst of it seemed to drift down from the top like so much corporate dandruff. As an employed writer, I can vividly recall such things as stopping in the midst of writing a major article to write a progress report on the article because someone in New York wanted "to have something in the files on the project, just in case."

There are limits to this line of soloist reasoning—many things do require collaboration and an organization—and there are times when the most independent of us take on a partner, or join a team, but it is an option, not an eternal given.

Another appealing element of the one-man or one-woman organization is the ultimate efficiency of not having to justify, explain and discuss what you are about to do before you do it. The independent can make the newly sainted "one minute manager" seem like an indecisive slowpoke. Ranging from sharpening a pencil to toying with a highly speculative idea in its most abstract form, all you have to do is decide it has to be done and you do it. There is a corresponding difficulty here which comes when you are an independent working with an organization and suddenly find the paperwork and the "call back" slips piling up. You find that your tolerance for all of this is not as great as it is among those who are part of the system.

Finally, there is the purely selfish consideration of not having to be considerate and civilized at all times. We can, on any given Monday morning, look at all those talk-show and self-help book verities—caring, sharing, dressing for success, being your own best friend—and say the hell with all of them. To be sure, there are times when you have to be able to charm birds out of trees and become the paragon of politeness, but not from 9 to 5 every day. Some of us work better and happier in a grubby sweatshirt, a halo of cigar smoke, a maelstrom of clutter or the vortex of all-rock radio—the very things that drive others bonkers. The point is that it is your pick and even more to the point is the fact that you can also pick the place and the time.

I work at home in a large comfortable office which was carefully designed, outfitted and financed by me. It is two rooms actually: one is the main room and it adjoins a library. It took a long time to work up to this place and I am still making improvements on it. As it stands, it is quiet, well lit, fully carpeted, a little cluttered, fairly efficient and very private.

Whatever coherence it has is completely personal. This allows me to work on a brand-new word processor while seated at an ancient swivel desk chair which, among other things, was once the property of the Maryland Fish and Game Commission and was used onstage in a production of *The Detective Story*. Because of its age, I must baby the chair a lot and from time to time must stop working to fix it after it throws one of its antique nuts or bolts because of a vigorous swivel. Because of the maintenance it requires, it is most inefficient and would have been banned from any place of employment years ago. It also makes a lot of noise, which comes in handy because when I am trying to get out of a long phone conversation I can make it sound like static on the line. I figure that whatever time I give up keeping it together, I more than make up for by getting out of phone marathons. I find it very hard to work in any other chair.

The feature I like most about it is that I work looking out a picture window into the trees.

At the beginning of the day, I enjoy coming into the place and on those occasions when I must work at night or on weekends I don't feel like a martyr. I can't imagine a place I would rather work, and when I see the sets where others work—determined by the tastes of designers, organized around some vague modular or "open office" principle, or given amenities which correlate with seniority or hierarchical position—I become doubly thankful.

Just as I can't imagine not being self-employed, it is hard to imagine that I could ever again work in one of those great glass and concrete boxes where the windows don't even open and you spend inordinately long periods of time waiting for elevators. I once worked on the 32nd floor of one of those climate-controlled monsters on Sixth Avenue in New York. It was dreadful then and more so in retrospect. What I hated most about it was being hermetically sealed in a place for eight climate-controlled hours a day where it felt and smelled the same on the first warm spring morning as it did during a snowstorm. To get near a window you had to have had your first ulcer.

There are some incidental disadvantages. From time to time I get the feeling of being housebound. This comes most often in the colder months when I may be putting in long hours at the typewriter. The feeling is most likely to hit late in the afternoon or on a weekend when no excursions are planned. The antidote is simple: get out of the house and relish the prospect of a list of errands to be run.

Then there is the problem of sometimes not being able to get away from work...sometimes you stumble back into it when you shouldn't and sometimes it happens when someone calls in the middle of Sunday afternoon or during dinner to discuss something you've been working on. For me, there are moments when the blessings of the telephone become hard to recall.

TIME ON MY SIDE

They say that time is money, but time is actually more important, or at least that is the way I have come to see it in my mid-40s. Given this, I am free to make decisions based on what they mean to me in terms of my time. Consider the following:

Retirement

I don't really plan to retire in the normal sense of the word, but I have made it my goal to work about one less week per year. In 1983 I did not work eight weeks, I took nine in 1984 and expect to hit double digits in 1985. I'm sure there will be years in which I deviate from the plan but the goal is clearly established and the whole idea brings me great pleasure. It is also amusing to me that when I have told people I am retiring a week a year, they often think that I'm kidding, that it is a throwaway line which I use to amuse people at cocktail parties.

The way I look at it is that under my plan I'll be working about half a year when I'm 65 while others will go from working 48 to 50 weeks a year when they are 64 to zero weeks a year when they hit the magic number, a radical shift that would not suit me at all. I also think that the half year I work at 65 will be a highly efficient and productive half year. Under my plan I'll be fully retired when I'm 87, which I figure is just about right.

I also find it genuinely sad to hear men and women of my age say that they are deferring dreams until their retirement at age 65 or maybe a couple of years earlier. People who talk like this tend to treat the latest life expectancy figures as a personal reality rather than a generalized probability.

All of this is not to say that I am not preparing for retirement. Each year I am putting away as much as I can in Keogh and IRA pension plans. What I will do in my 60s is to begin taking money out of those plans as I work the equivalent of a half year.

Daily Work

Many years ago, when I was in high school, I decided that one of the reigning absurdities of the 40-hour, five-day workweek was that it was the same in February as it was in August. I dreamt of being able to work seasonally but figured that I would have to scuttle the idea as part of the payment for growing up unless I wanted to become a professional snow shoveler.

From the beginning of my self-employment I have seasonally adjusted my schedule to take advantage of the months, becoming a quasi-workaholic in the winter and easing off when it is nice out. I can't imagine a better way to schedule work. So much for the dues of adulthood.

This plan is not ironclad as there have been times of goofing off in the winter and hard work in the summer, but the general gist of the idea has remained intact. I think I have averaged something just over 40 hours a week in the last few years and was averaging a little more than that five years ago.

I rarely work a standard 9 to 5 day and have long lost any traces of guilt over not starting by 10 A.M. or taking the afternoon off to take a ride in the country. I can easily reel off a long list of great moments enjoyed on weekday afternoons when by conventional standards "I should have been working." More often than not, I have banked some time—dug in for a Friday night or whenever—against a free afternoon.

Without going into some cloying comments on "fathering," I can say that this daily freedom has given me a great deal of important time with my two children during the day. Before they started going to school full time, I was able to grab time to be with them and now I am home most days to greet them when school is over. We have gone sleigh riding when school was canceled because of snow and we have all been at home for an afternoon talk about what went on in school on a particular day. Over time this freedom to act as a true family member is something that does not get taken for granted. If anything, it seems to become more and more important and something to be protected with greater zeal. For instance, one does not have to be a child psychologist to know that young children attach a great deal of importance to Halloween. For that reason I have doggedly kept that day free of meetings, trips and other adult activities so I can watch the kids march in their Halloween parade, an event I have never missed nor ceased to enjoy.

While on the subject of children, I should point out that I am often asked by other parents how I can work at home with kids around. The answer is fairly easily. Both children, now six and ten, were born into a home where I was working and to them it is the norm. From time to time there has been a bad moment as a sibling tussle or an attack of the whines broke out during an important phone call (one actually when I was talking to a senator whom I'd been trying to get to talk to for weeks), but for the most part it has been a sheer delight to have them around when I'm at work as they have learned to limit their interruptions.

At this point in my life, I actually dread the day when they are off at college or wherever and that at least part of my working day is not spent with them around. I'll miss that moment in the day when they come in from school with a sudden gust of news, plans, gossip and complaints about how bad lunch was. To me it is a daily ritual with as much importance as a leisurely dinner with rambling family conversation.

Another aspect of this that I have never taken for granted took place during the time that my father was sick and dying. Quite simply, as I was in full possession of the right to my own time, I was able to be with him for many days. I did not have to ask anyone for time off, calculate how many vacation days I had left or experience any of the humiliations that I would have had to experience as an employee. If I had been encumbered by a regular job at that time, there would have been a very good chance that I would have had to quit to get the time I needed. To say that it was important to have control at that time of my life and my father's life is to indulge in understatement. To this day, that block of time remains the beacon which reminds me that no cornucopia of employee benefits can possibly measure up to the self-employed benefit of control over one's own sacred, sweet time.

AT PLAY IN THE FIELDS OF WORK

Leisure Time

Perhaps this is not as true of some self-employed professions as others, but I have found that there are times when work and play seem to blend and become inseparable. When these distinctions blur, I find myself about as far removed from the traditional realm of 9 to 5 work as imaginable.

Let me give an example. In 1971 I was finishing a book and started looking around for historic photographs to illustrate it with. The search led me to a variety of photographic archives including the Prints and Photographs Division of the Library of Congress. Before the search was over I had become totally fascinated with old photographs and was soon collecting them and reading all I could on the subject. I wrote articles on the subject and—as my interest grew to include certain aspects of modern photography—wrote a book on space photography which was published in 1977. It was done as a labor of love and sold a respectable number of copies.

At this point, I'm working on several photographic projects. For instance, I am collecting the work of and facts about an obscure but brilliant 19th century photographer named M. A. Kleckner whom I am planning to eventually write a book about. It is a low-priority project which I come back to at odd moments, especially when I want to escape to another time and place through this man's remarkable pictures. It will take years of odd moments to complete this project and I know even at this point that it will have severely limited commercial potential. To be perfectly frank, I'm not even sure that it will work because of the difficulty in getting facts on the subject.

In all of this I wouldn't even try to figure out whether I was, at a particular moment, working or playing with a hobby. For this reason, there is virtually nothing that I can get involved in that can't be turned into "work" in the form of a book or magazine article. This blurred distinction between work and play is not only true of writers but I've heard the same from people in fields as diverse as landscaping and antique dealing.

This works as well for things I must do. A few years ago, I was called to jury duty, representing days of unpaid work save for a small meal stipend of $15 a day. Everyone else on the jury was either retired or fully salaried and was being paid for the days they served on the jury. I turned this around by writing a magazine article about the jury system in question which netted me $750. I know of at least two other writers who have done the same thing and wonder if the market for stories on jury duty won't soon be saturated.

Annual Considerations

As a self-employed person, I have chosen to approach my work in annual January to December increments. This fits in with the rest of the world, the IRS among others, and lets me set goals accordingly. At the end of each year I list the major things I hope to accomplish during the year and continually update the list during the year. Something which seemed important at the beginning of the year may not seem so important in August and be dropped, while something else may crop up—an opportunity not imagined at the beginning of the year—to replace it. Trading goals like this is often most satisfying when you can "bait and switch"—dropping a lesser idea for a new, top-of-the-line notion.

I point this out to show that this form of work can gain some degree of coherence, yet remain flexible. Failures notwithstanding, I have found that this is a most workable and satisfactory way to set goals. Again, the beauty of the system derives from the fact that you are in control, with nobody else setting your priorities and quotas. Of course,there are limits to the flexibility. Because most of my income comes from writing books, each year must have a completed book-length manuscript in it as the prime goal.

Another nice thing about this annual system is that it lets me indulge in setting goals which have nothing to do with making a living or the ubiquitous "bottom line." They are not tax deductible, have nothing to do with the common good and fly in the face of all that is deemed efficient.

To give a top-of-the-line example, a few years ago it occurred to me that it would be great fun to see if I could get into the *Guinness Book of World Records*. What this quest represented purely and simply was the adolescent fantasy of setting a record and had nothing whatsoever to do with business. Such a goal would have been deemed heresy in a corporate job and to have sought it during working hours would have been just cause for my dismissal. On the average I put one or two of these offbeat goals on the list each year and take the greatest delight in knowing they are there for the pure fun of it.

Beyond the year in question, I dabble in five-year plans in which I tentatively pencil in long-range plans. These distant plans tend to be rough and help give me some perspective on where I'm going and where I've been.

MONEY MATTERS

The major failures which I have experienced in this area have mostly been financial goals. For several years in the 1970s I wrote down as a goal "Gross $30,000" and for several years running I wrote "failed" after the goal. Then for 1977 I wrote "Gross $30,000 or get out." I missed by more than $7,000 and didn't even momentarily consider getting out, although on several occasions I told people I thought anyone who became self-employed had a screw loose. In 1978 I didn't list any financial goals and went over the long-targeted $30,000.

Speaking of money, there were two points earlier in my freelance career when I felt that I was making so little money that I would indeed have to give up, but didn't. There was nothing especially noble about going on as it was really a function of selfishly not wanting to give up the freedom I had claimed for myself. On both occasions something came along which put enough bucks in the bank to end the crisis. One of these amounted to a $10,000 windfall arranged by my agent who found investors to buy an interest in one of my books as a tax shelter. It was a dazzling moment which was the personal equivalent of the corporate bailouts of Lockheed and Chrysler.

Financially, I have bad years, fair years, a number of good years and one that was excellent. However, the only way I will ever hit six figures gross will be through a remarkable piece of luck or through the kind of inflation that would bring us $3.75 ice cream cones and $12.00 movies. Like most self-employed people I am content to have an occasional dream about a big hit, but never to be seduced by the idea—to actually believe it will happen. Like all writers, I know that there is nothing to prevent me, with nothing more than a typewriter and a box of paper, from coming up with a blockbuster book which will bring me a million dollars in royalties. It's fun to think about but it is something like the flip side to being hit by a truck: you know it could happen but don't believe it will happen to you.

To put this into a different perspective, I have kept close enough to sources in the employed world and have had enough job offers to be able to say that, on the average, I have not fared as well as I would have had I stuck it out as an employed Washington journalist or editor. I'm told by those in the know that the rule of thumb for successful journalists hereabouts is to be making one and half times your age (up from the time—not that long ago—when success was defined as "making your age"). In 1983, for instance, my gross income was fairly close to the 1.5 age multiple, but my net came quite close to my age. Compare this net to someone making their age for a corporation and figure in that they are, on the average, getting benefits worth 35% of their income. In actual dollars the average American employee, according to the U.S. Chamber of Commerce, got $7,187 per year or $138 per week in benefits from his or her employer.

Consider then that the average employee is making salary plus $7,187. In order to achieve parity the self-employed person must subtract that $7,187 from their gross. But it amounts to more than that because the bulk of those benefits are paid for in dollars which are taxed. Consider also that the self-employed must pay for all of his or her expenses from paper clips to photocopy machines. Roughly speaking, it is hard to be self-employed and not pay out a minimum of 20% of one's gross in expenses. In many cases, it goes much higher.

From time to time, I have been offered a position with a company as a writer—or as the person offering the job usually puts it, "How would you like a real job?" Because of the 1.5 times one's age formula I usually cut off these conversations with a polite turn-down before the issue of money comes up. By now I know that I won't take the job no matter what the offer is and knowing how much I'm being offered would just depress me.

I'm convinced that one of the things which throws others off when they think about self-employed people is that they often think of the gross and not the net. They hear of a writer getting a $100,000 advance on a book which will take the writer two years to write or hear of a mom and pop mail-order firm having sales of $250,000 and think of these as huge sums, which they are not. People who have never been outside a system with built-in benefits have a tendency to forget their worth.

An example of this kind of thinking can also get into the politics of self-employment. For me this was underscored during the 1972 presidential campaign when George McGovern announced the tax reforms which would take place when he took office. He stressed again and again that reform would not increase the tax burden of those who "depend on wages and salaries for their income."

To give him the benefit of the doubt, he probably meant he was going to go after bond coupon clippers and the richest surgeons, but he never made that clear. As a result he gave the impression that the chairman of the board of ITT whose 1972 salary was $812,494 or the head of Ford who was making $702,000 a year in salary was not to be touched but that an unsalaried, independent cab driver making $10,000 or the capitalistic owner of a barbershop making $15,000 was in for a shellacking. In fact, the first time I ever heard about this aspect of the McGovern tax plan was from a cabbie convinced that he would be nailed by it if McGovern got in. At the time, I thought that the irony of it all was that the very people most perplexed by McGovern's pledge to protect only wage and salaried workers were people like barbers, hairdressers, cabbies and waitresses who had a lot of contact with the public. It probably didn't bother the richer self-employed because they knew that they could always incorporate and let the corporation pay them a salary.

Ironically, I'm a bona fide die-hard Democrat who not only voted for McGovern but worked as a volunteer in his campaign. But on matters of self-employment I am a Republican. It is the Democrats who love to talk about the importance of the independent worker and the small business but who actually come down on the other side when it comes to action. Perhaps the best single example of this came in the early days of the Keogh retirement plans for the self-employed. Keogh plans were strongly and steadfastly opposed by both the Kennedy and Johnson administrations yet embraced by the Nixon and Ford administrations. (In fairness, the Eisenhower Treasury Department was opposed to the original legislation.)

PERKS AND BENES

All of this brings us back to the matter of benefits which represent a vast gulf between the employed and the self-employed. The first few years of my self-employment were years in which I spent a lot of time getting over the shock of not having things like health insurance and paid holidays, to say nothing of those perks which don't show up in employee benefit manuals—unlimited access to a photocopy machine, extended lunch hours, WATS lines and the like.

Unquestionably, my biggest shock was health and major medical insurance, which I had taken for granted. I was part of a group benefit plan which covered almost everything and for which I only had to pay less than half the cost, with the rest being paid for by my employer. Before that I had been covered by another employer, before that by the U.S. Navy, before that by a blanket system as a college student and before that as my father's dependent. I had grown up thinking that health and medical insurance was a given of American life, akin to freedom of religion.

I somehow thought that I would be able to buy something as good on the open market for just a little bit more. I was dreaming.

To spare all the details, I have had to spend much time and energy—and tens of thousands of U.S. dollars—to keep a minimal level of coverage. There have been times when I have had no coverage and known for months on end that a catastrophe—a bad disease, a debilitating automobile accident—would have wiped me out financially. The terror of those uncovered times was compounded by the fact that affordable disability insurance was also unavailable. It took a long time for me to realize the extent to which this was going to be a continuing burden. I kept thinking that I had somehow missed a simple solution, that it was a simple matter of finding the right door to knock on. What kept throwing me was that everybody I talked to in the insurance business wanted to sell me life insurance. If they could make money on the possibility of my death, I reasoned, why couldn't they do the same for illness or injury?

When the severity of the problem finally hit home, I thought that I would never have made the leap if I had understood the reality of the situation.

In the years since I left a corporate plan, I have had five different plans which have all tended to be too expensive and riddled with gaping exemptions. Three plans were canceled by the carrier and one simply became unaffordable. At the point when my first son was born, we were not covered for pregnancy and, like others in our situation, were forced to pay the hospital in advance in cash (it wouldn't even accept a check) in order to have a baby. Ironically, if I had had insurance at that point, the hospital—by the admission of the financial department—would not have been reimbursed for months.

That experience had its side effects. Because of the costs involved in an extended stay in the maternity ward, we were in and out of the hospital in less than 24 hours and when the final accounting was made with the hospital I found myself questioning and fighting items on the bill. I successfully got them to knock off a lab fee for a lab which had not been used and for disposable diapers which had been clearly marked a gift from the manufacturer. I failed, however, to get them to readjust charges for specific drug store items which were billed at two or three times their retail price at the drug store around the corner. All this haggling drove home the vast gulf between our situation and those with "full boat" coverage who don't even get to see their bills in most cases as they go directly to Blue Cross or whomever.

Nowhere is it written that America's insurance industry *has* to insure the self-employed. For many, the only answer lies in using larger groups and associations to buy insurance on a group basis, but this is not as easy as it may seem. Insurers like to offer what they term "group" insurance to groups but then reserve the right to reject those which they think are too risky—individuals and families with a chronic illness, a disease in remission, a history of cancer or whatever. The use of the term "group" in these cases is a cruel deception and a genuinely fraudulent use of the term.

The barrier erected by the fact that there is no legal provision for making sure that all self-employed must be able to buy some sort of health insurance is enough to keep some out of self-employment permanently. A friend and neighbor, Dr. Fitzhugh Mullan, who wrote about his successful fight with cancer in his book *Vital Signs*, said in that book he might never be able to go back to private practice because his history of cancer would make him uninsurable.

Ironically, those in the insurance industry who have fought so diligently against any form of national health insurance take no responsibility for those who now fall between the actuarial cracks.

As of this writing, I am thankfully covered by a group called the Maryland Individual Practice Association. It ain't cheap—over $2,800 a year—but it works and it is a lot cheaper than the last plan I had, which was closing in on $4,000 a year. Based on past experience, however, I must always keep other options in mind as I have seen other plans fall apart and am confident that the system will again find a way to spit me out and that I will have to hustle once again for insurance. I have accepted it as a depressing fact of self-employed life.

REP. EUGENE KEOGH'S PLAN

Although insurance is a sore sticking point of self-employment, there is another side of the benefit gulf which has been closing since the passage in 1962 of a bill by former Rep. Eugene Keogh (D, N.Y.) allowing the self-employed to set aside a percentage, initially 10% of income up to $2,500, of their income tax free and put it in their own pension plan. Once retired, the individual can take the money out, paying taxes on it as retirement income. Prior to this, the self-employed could only save after-tax dollars while corporate and government employees were able to shelter their contributions from taxes.

Looking back on what took place between the day in 1951 when Keogh and Rep. Daniel Reed (who died before it was passed) first proposed the legislation and its final passage in 1962 is instructional. It shows the extent of the struggle by the self-employed to gain this right. Through those years there were countless Congressional hearings on the matter during which the self-employed literally begged for an end to, as the president of the American Bar Association put it, "this discrimination against the self-employed." Every possible angle was

44

ON OUR OWN

studied including equivalent plans in effect in Great Britain, Canada
and New Zealand. Supporting the bill, H.R. 10, was a motley lot of
professional groups—dentists, farmers, writers, independent
insurance agents and realtors, ranchers, accountants, ornamental
horticulturalists—as well as the banks which looked forward to
providing a place to keep those retirement funds.

Despite all of this, the bill went nowhere as a powerful coalition
spoke out against it. One force was the Treasury Department,
representing the Eisenhower Administration, which saw it as
"substantial loss of revenue" that would further deepen the national
debt by cutting the tax base. Others fighting it ranged from the National
Education Association to individual legislators who, to quote one of
them, believed, "The people who will get the real advantage and the
real tax break under this proposal are those in the extremely high
income tax bracket."

Organized labor was deeply opposed. The AFL-CIO's Peter Henle
working to defeat the bill in 1959 told a Senate committee, "We are
here to oppose this bill in the most vigorous terms. We believe that
H.R. 10 represents special interest legislation providing tax benefits
for a relatively few in our population; that it does not correct any
existing inequity in our tax laws, but helps to create new ones; and that
it would deprive the U.S. Treasury of much needed revenue in 1960
and future years." Labor not only argued that this would have a
crippling effect on the revenue system, but that the self-employed
"already receive many specific tax advantages." The union pushed the
idea that the self-employed were not reporting all their income to the
IRS but the "individual worker or salaried person" had no such
opportunity.

The irony of it all was that those who opposed it most strongly were
those with pensions—Federal, corporate, municipal or
whatever—which the self-employed were helping to pay for. Moss
Hart, then president of the Authors League of America, told the
Senate Finance Committee in 1961, "...the present situation is not
simply a matter of the self-employed being denied a privilege which
the employed now have. Self-employed taxpayers are now being
required, in effect, to help finance and pay for the retirement of
employed taxpayers. If the hundreds of millions of dollars which are
annually paid into retirement funds for corporate employees were not
tax deductible, then the Treasury would receive millions in taxes from
this source; an increase which would permit an overall reduction in
tax rates or, at least, cut down further increases, thus benefiting the
self-employed taxpayer."

H.R. 10 was finally passed in 1962 as a severely watered-down and
restriction-laden version of the original. It went into effect in 1964 and

was, to use the term used by Steven Anreder in his book *Retirement Dollars for the Self-Employed*, a dud. "There were so many restrictions put on self-employed retirement plans that it hardly paid for a person to tie up his money," Anreder wrote, "In 1964...more than 10,500 plans were approved by the Internal Revenue Service. Two years later the number had actually declined to 7,500." Less than a million dollars a year was going into the nation's Keogh plans while billions continued to go into employee plans. The loss in revenues amounted to a few hundred thousand dollars a year, a far cry from the hundreds of millions being forecast by the Treasury Department before the bill was passed.

Strongly opposed by Presidents Kennedy and Johnson, who still felt it would be too much of a drain on tax revenues, it stayed in place as a complicated dud wrapped in red tape and restrictions. Starting with a liberalization in 1968, it became more attractive and a little less complicated, but it was still a world apart from corporate plans. It finally came into its own with President Nixon's proposed boost to 15% of one's income or $7,500, whichever was less—up from a maximum of $2,500 a year—and was passed by both houses of Congress by a whopping majority as part of a larger pension-reform package. It was signed into law by President Ford on Labor Day, 1974. At the beginning of 1984 a further liberalization allowed higher limits which gave the self-employed the same ability to put away retirement dollars as those who are incorporated.

The official IRS name for the Keogh plan is an H.R. 10 plan, but I try not to use that term for ideological reasons. Keeping Congressman Keogh's name in place is a reminder that one man effected a change that helped make it possible for many to become self-employed. Nobody actually knows how many decided to make the leap because of the Keogh option, but few would question the statement that it has been a major factor. Although I didn't make enough money in the first few years of self-employment to start a plan, I did get one started and have since worked hard to get as much into it as I could afford. It is a major cushion in my self-employment and something which I doubt I will ever take for granted.

Because of the flexibility built into the Keogh rules, I have been able to invest and reinvest the money in bonds, certificates of deposit, growth stocks and occasionally something decidedly speculative. Tending the account has been fun and I enjoy being my own pension manager. With the help of a good broker, I've done pretty well as the successful investments have far outnumbered the few bad ones. I've also learned that you don't do this in a vacuum as it has meant keeping an eye on the financial pages of the paper.

The modicum of security which comes with having your own

pension brings up the larger issue of overall security. It is hard for me
to recall a conversation that I've had with an employed person about
self-employment which did not eventually get around to this issue. At
some point in the conversation the employed person usually says that
they could not live with the insecurity of work outside of an institution.
Ironically, I vividly remember two of the people who made this point
were subsequently fired, laid off or, as they now put it in some circles,
outplaced.

Over time, I have concluded that what some people see as job
security is an elusive commodity which moves like quicksilver in and
out of the realms of the real and the imagined. I have been under
contract with publishers which have ordered wholesale layoffs, had
editors axed in the middle of projects and had assignments from
magazines which disappeared from the face of the earth before I
reached my deadline. Watching all of this, I have realized the
importance of being in a position where you can't be tossed aside and
treated, as most employees are ultimately, as a variable expense and
temporary resource. I am constantly reminded that almost all
employers maintain the right to get rid of people as one of their most
cherished and unchallengable rights.

Because I make most of my money through books, I now own
practically all that I write. This means I am paid through a royalty
system which has deficiencies but which keeps paying me as long as my
books still sell. Recently, I got a small royalty check from a book which
was first published in 1972 and which has paid at least something each
year since it came out. Such things add up to give you your own sense
of security. You know it is an imperfect and flawed sense of security
but it beats standing naked in the world without one...and in its own
way it is incomparably better than a system in which you don't have
control over what you produce.

Ironically, the strongest sense of security I have ever gotten from
owning what I produce first came wrapped as a failure. I had written a
book and soon after it came out, it was clear that people were avoiding
it to the extent that I was hard pressed to find another book which was
failing quite so dramatically. I hunted for a metaphor that would
convey it all and found it at the zoo, where I saw a sign pointing out
how few people are actually bitten by poisonous snakes each year in
the United States. The number was higher than the first year's sales
for the book, making it more likely that your average American would
have been bitten by a poisonous snake than he would have bought the
book. Henceforth and forever, it was my "snake-bite" book.

After accepting the failure, a funny thing began happening. Through
my agent the book started to attract interest outside the United States,
and before I knew it, there were editions in Japanese, German and

French, and a British publisher brought out both hardcover and paperback editions. The money involved was not great but it was enough to move it out of the pile marked failure and into the pile marked moderately successful. Then as now, the experience led me to the conclusion that when you are on your own you have more opportunities to effect that old chestnut about seeing victory snatched from the jaws of defeat. In this case, victory came through a mix of luck and persistence on the part of my agent, but the fact that it was a good book had something to do with it. I realize that humility did not dictate that opinion, but to this day I am still convinced that that snake-bite book was the best one I ever wrote.

The experience of the snake-bite book also made it easier to rid myself of the traditional notion of success and failure. I was beginning to learn what I presume many other self-employed have come to realize and that is that you are allowed to label your own achievements or, if you prefer, decide to de-emphasize the conventional distinction between success and failure. In the *Washintgon Post*, writer and entrepreneur Mary E. Ames put it most directly, "The self-employed person is uniquely in a position to define success however he pleases." This is not to say that there is not a deep sense of the extremes—grand slam home runs *vs.* strikeouts—but a lot of what falls in between is yours to interpret as you like. To continue the baseball analogy, there is no reason to lament a beautiful line drive that gets caught at the wall.

BOLLES' FALLACY

Some would argue with this declaration of independence and personal freedom. Richard Bolles, author of the perennial best-seller *What Color is Your Parachute?*, also writes a newsletter. He devoted one issue of that newsletter to the subject of self-employment and in that issue much space to the "fallacy of being self-employed" in which he said, "There is a very real sense in which self-employment is largely a myth. Technically, the only genuinely self-employed person is one who has an independent income, or one who lives on his or her own food, and is able to procure by barter or trade all of the services he or she needs." He goes on to say that everyone else actually works for someone else and is therefore an employee of one or more employers, adding that seeking self-employment is "really a job-hunt in disguise."

Bolles' point is well taken in the sense that almost all of us are dependent on others to pay us for what we do, but that hardly qualifies as a fact which destroys the myth of independence. I maintain that it is not a myth at all but a day to day reality which allows us latitude and freedom that very few employed people ever enjoy. If anything, there are times when so many options are open that one wistfully thinks back to the days when you came to work and somebody told you what to do or an established policy pointed you in a specific direction. Bolles sees the myth as one which is harbored by those contemplating self-employment, but those who have made the leap are those who stick with it for the simple reason that it is not a myth.

The freedom is a given and so is the dependence on other people and factors—intermediaries, buyers, the IRS, the changing body of law and regulation, the national and regional economy, bank loan officers, agents, accountants, lawyers and too many others to mention.

Yet with the seeming cast of thousands whom you depend on, there is the freedom to change direction, the freedom to say no to a project because you don't believe in it, the freedom to not work for somebody for whatever reason, the freedom from policy which has been set by someone else, the freedom from the kind of failure where someone must be blamed before the books can be closed, the freedom from pink slips, "outplacement counselors" and forced early retirement.

If one needs a myth or two to poke a few holes in, one is that of total, laid-back freedom from the demands of a boss. Dr. J. M. Rathbun, a self-employed psychiatrist, has put it succinctly and correctly in his *First Law of Self-Employment*: "There is no harder nor more thankless taskmaster than the self-employed." The fact is that you are quite likely to go through periods in which you drive yourself to such a degree that if you were a boss and were driving an employee in a place of business you'd be facing criminal charges for violation of all sorts of laws. There are times when you force yourself to work below the minimum wage, violate all the overtime rules and generally exhibit the compassion of a sweatshop foreman in a particularly nasty mood.

The other myth in need of debunking is that self-employed work is not work. To be sure there are times when it is the most pleasurable work one can imagine, but that is not to say that it does not conform to the classic definition of work: taking responsibility for a certain task for a certain length of time, which in most cases means that some of it is going to be tedious, boring and uncomfortable. It is interesting to note that some of the people who have worked long and hard to make factory and office work more interesting and give workers more and more decision-making responsibilities have learned that there are limits to the improvements that can be made. Harry Levinson, writing about this in *The Levinson Letter*, said that "many people have come to expect too much of work, work is work no matter how you slice it..."

Despite the boss's inhumanity and the nature of work itself, the freedoms remain. In addition, for me at least, there was another freedom, that of being free from the assumptions which I had made and which had been made for me as I grew up. In school, things were always discussed in terms of jobs, and who you would go to work for. Guidance counselors talked about employed careers, and when you were a senior in college there were three major options: graduate school, the military or a job with a corporation or government. The subject of self-employment didn't even come up, and if you wanted to talk with someone about the future, there were a number of recruiters who would gladly set up an appointment to see you.

INVALID ASSUMPTIONS

For me, the assumption had always been that I would eventually gravitate into working for a large corporation. After a few corporate interviews as a college senior, I realized that I had better defer such a move for as long as possible. What got to me more than anything else was the fact that all the recruiters stressed pension plans and retirement. At 21, the last thing on my mind was my financial security in the next century. I would become 65 in the year 2004 and in 1961, when I graduated from college, for all I cared they could ship my aging bones to a rest home on Mars.

With the full knowledge that I would be giving up pension credits, I took off for a year in Europe, working half that time for a small Swedish shipping company. During those months in Sweden I met a number of people my own age and some of them seemed overly infatuated with the lifetime of security promised them in a corporation within a socialist society. The substance and style of what one was going to do for the next 45 years seemed less important than the support system that came with it: the guaranty had become more important than the product itself.

After that, I again deferred the inevitable by going into the Navy as a reserve officer. Toward the end of that three-year stint, I was approached by my executive officer who tried to convince me that I should make a full career of the Navy—after all, he pointed out, where else could I retire securely after only 20 years.

As an easy retirement seemed to be the main selling point in the discussion, I came out of it with the same feeling that had been planted by the college recruiters—ending your career seemed to be one of the prime goals of having one. I could see it for someone who was going to spend their working life in a dank coal mine or watching traffic in an exhaust-filled tunnel, but not for me. It all seemed too well packaged, like a foreign tour in which everything, including rest room stops, is scheduled. In a way the Navy's "20 and out" plan was the most unsettling because it meant that I'd be heading out to pasture in my early 40s, a point at which I figured should ideally be when an adult hits full working stride. It was as odd to me as being told that if you became a parent that you could unload your kids when they became teenagers.

Ironically, if I had taken the Navy up on its offer, I would have become retired at just about the time I am writing this. The notion is appalling because I feel that I have just recently become truly comfortable with what I am doing, have a fairly good idea of my strengths and weaknesses and have at least a vague awareness of the rules of the game I've chosen to play. What's more, I am now enjoying what I'm doing as much or more than I ever have, yet I still do a lot of experimenting and tinkering with what I do. I now know that if I had just retired, it would have been in name only because I'd be struggling with a second career at this very moment.

Furthermore, if the idea of having retired at 44 is appalling, so too is the idea of facing full retirement at 54 or 64 because, barring illness or injury, I know that my energy and fascination with what I'm doing would make it a silly, self-defeating gesture, like walking out of a play in the middle of the third act.

I admit that I have been enormously influenced in this matter by my father, who looked upon retirement as something for the elderly, who were always defined as people older than himself. In fact, he achieved his greatest success in life after 65, when he became the president of a major New York bank, and worked full time up until he became terminally ill at age 73. In fact, he worked until he was too sick to continue. I always admired the fact that he had found something that he really liked doing and saw no reason to stop doing just because he was over 65. He was not a workaholic, but neither was he a man destined to retire. Writing has always had the special appeal of something that you don't retire from. You may want to ease off some, but you don't leave it like you leave the mines, or the government or the phone company. As I write this, a writer I know has just headed off to Florida with a nice magazine assignment. His name is Howard Bloomfield and he is 84.

After I left the Navy and its generous retirement offer, I decided that I should spend a year in Spain where I could live on the money I had put aside during the last three years. I took courses, watched a lot of bullfights and did some writing. I had started writing travel articles in the Navy and had been successful selling them to the likes of the *New York Times, New York Herald Tribune* and *Saturday Review*. I kept this up in Spain and started other projects including a children's book. After this delightful year, I returned to New York, where I thought the newspapers would be fighting over a chance to hire me. Unfortunately, this was a time when newspapers were folding and merging and the market was glutted with journalists. After knocking on as many possible doors as I could find, including those of the most obscure trade magazines, I gave up and signed up with a leading brokerage house to train to become an account executive, a fancy term for a person who buys and sells stocks for his customers.

It was all very exciting to begin with and I was near the top of my group of trainees. My high standing in the class was my undoing because on the eve of my becoming a full-fledged account executive I was taken aside by the man who was to be my manager and, with no little ceremony, was given a specialty. A specialty was not a group of stocks, but rather a type of person each novice was assigned to by the manager. One was expected to contact, attract and learn to deal with this group—which was to be the nucleus of your business. Because of my standing in the class, I was rewarded with a prize while my peers were given prosaic groups like taxi fleet owners and New Jersey dentists. The prize specialty was recently widowed women and I was promised that by the time I was assigned to a desk in the branch office I would be given a long typewritten list recently culled from the obituary pages. I quit the next morning and the prize was awarded to a fellow who, I was told, accepted it with ghoulish good humor.

Back at square one, I started looking for a writing job again and with the help of a personnel agency got a job with a big publishing house in its public relations department. The company published a number of trade magazines, and I figured, correctly, that if I got a job in the company I could eventually finagle my way into a spot as a magazine writer. This took less than a year and I found myself in the position of a staff writer for a magazine covering the electronics industry. I knew nothing about electronics but that didn't matter. I was writing and learning a lot in the process. I was also lucky to have landed with a magazine which covered what was then and still is America's most dynamic industry.

I worked for this magazine for five years, time that was about as well spent as I could have hoped. The time amounted to a graduate school in journalism and writing during which I was able to develop interests that I could later exploit in books and magazine articles. One of the nice things about the job was that I was assigned to write about subjects which I knew little or nothing about. There were a number of nights which were spent in the library reading up on a subject like lasers so that I could spend the next morning talking to some of the leading experts in the field. I found a certain exhilaration in being thrown in over my head.

But in all of this there was a corporate assumption that I did not share. It was that I would eventually rise to an executive job as a bureau chief or senior editor. I was told that my destiny was to become a boss and that with any luck I would soon be working on vacation schedules and writing fine memos on the importance of getting expense accounts submitted before the 10th of the month. Then one day when I was offered such a position, I turned it down and was told that it would not be in my best interests to turn down a second promotion when it came along. The first offer was for a job in San Francisco and I doubted that the second one would take me to a place even half as nice.

What I began to realize was that on this major point and a lot of others, my interests and those of the company were vastly different. Somewhere in the back of my mind I always knew that I would eventually head off in my own direction and the time to do it was at hand. Part of it was my desire to get out of a system of being bossed and being a boss, and the other part was to be able to develop as a writer without the clear and present danger of a promotion and the curse of a title. I did, however, want to keep getting myself in over my head; but I'd just as soon do the pushing myself.

There was one other small point. I felt that I wasn't being paid what I was worth. Some of it had to do with the fact that I had come into the company at the lowest acceptable salary, $5,300 a year, and the raises I had gotten were good percentage raises but didn't amount to much in real take-home dollars. One of the most irksome things about this was that I was producing more than some people who were getting a lot more money. This was not contested by the management, which told me what it told others in the same position: raises were gradual and seniority had its rewards. Doubly irksome was the fact that one day I was picked to have lunch with a man about to graduate from journalism school and convince him to come work for the company. It was a jolly lunch and I was doing a fine recruiting job, but it all fell apart when the fellow told me how much he had been offered to start. He would get more for his first week than I was getting per week after three years. I politely cut off the lunch to call New York to tell the man who had set up the lunch that he had been crazy to put us together. The man in New York told me that I had been foolish to start as low as I had. Ironically, I was given a really nice raise at the point I announced that I was moving on.

As it turned out, I heard about and got hold of a fellowship which supported me for a year in which I could take courses, travel and do the bulk of the work on my first book. Although I never worked so hard in one year before or after, it was a glorious way to make the shift. I was one of the fortunate few who was subsidized while changing gears.

PERMANENT SHIFT

I bring all of this up to underscore the fact that I was led into self-employment by assumptions made by others...that retirement is a major force in planning your life...that job security is more important than the job...that all adult Americans who go to college and have a firm handshake are destined to manage...and that money is the great motivator even if it comes from commissions generated by the recently widowed. Looking back on it from the higher ground of middle age, the assumptions seem just as invalid as they seemed when I first realized they were being made for me. Ironically, they were all being made by people who thought they were doing the right thing for me and I've always appreciated this. It was just a simple matter of those assumptions being wrong.

Having now been self-employed since the days when you could mail a first-class letter for six cents and this month's Playmate of the Month was still watching *Sesame Street*, I know that the shift was inevitable and is now permanent. I rather enjoy the fact that the assumptions which the corporate world would now make for me will soon exclude me from that world forever. I am at or nearing that age when the climb up the ladder would make little sense and any personnel officer worth his or her salt would look at what I've been up to for all these years and correctly conclude that this is a person with no interest in writing the great American inter-departmental memo, who would probably do everything within his power to avoid staff meetings and who doesn't need an office Christmas party to get him in the holiday mood. Although going back is now inconceivable, I actually could see myself dabbling in other forms of self-employment, probably in the form of some sort of small family enterprise.

MISTAKEN IDENTITY

Something which has long bothered me is the difficulty in getting a good picture of the people who are self-employed in the United States. Beyond the basic fact of how many millions of us there are and the continuing announcements that the total is going up, it is hard to get a picture of what we really do to put bread on the table, how old we are and what made us do it in the first place.

Such information is not just a curiosity. It helps give self-employment an identity and it tends to work against a negative mythology which seems to have cropped up around elements of self-employment.

A case in point is that for years I read and heard that only a handful of people were "making it" as freelance writers in the United States. An article in *Newsday* in 1978 contained the estimate that "there are probably fewer than 300 people in this country who make a living at freelance writing." *The Washington Post* used the same figure and it appeared in *Time*, which attributed it to a journalism school dean who concluded that some 25,000 citizens call themselves freelance writers "but fewer than 300 make a living at it." It got to the point where this "statistic" haunted me and even other writers were quoting it to me. It bothered me because it seemed like a barrier in itself, a way of saying you're crazy to even think about such a thing. I was thankful that I had not started when this "fewer than 300" was being bandied about.

The number, of course, is an absurdity mindlessly repeated by those who never bother to check the figure. Not only can I actually name more than 300 (which I did one night with the help of another writer) but a local group which I belong to, Washington Independent Writers, has 1,400 members of whom more than 400 are full-time freelance writers. Nor are these folks marginally self-employed as the group's 1983 membership survey indicated their average annual income was $26,100. In addition, there are probably another hundred in the area who are not members.

Much more dramatic, however, are the latest figures from the Bureau of Labor Statistics which say that in 1983 there were 47,000 self-employed authors in the United States as well as 1,000 self-employed technical writers and 13,000 self-employed editors and reporters. The BLS, by the way, only counts a person once in a single profession, so these are not people who sell storm windows all day and write on the side. Either the 300 figure is off or 60,700 people are lying to the government about what they do for a living.

Such mythology is harmful. And there is a lot more of it including those oft-quoted "statistics" on the tremendous failure rate of new businesses. One which recently showed up in my local newspaper asserted that "95% of all new businesses in the United States fail," while others take the more conservative line that more than 65% fail in the first five years. Ohio State University Professor Albert Shapero, who collects such "statistics," wrote of them in *Inc.* magazine: "One of the biggest barriers to entrepreneurship is the widespread notion that almost all new businesses fail in very short order. This myth discourages young people who might think of going into business for themselves, and it influences important people who affect start-ups...Why start a business when you know you're doomed to fail?" Shapero concludes, "The fact is that no one knows the start-up rate or the failure rate."

If vague notions and goofy statistics tend to attach themselves to independents, the same cannot be said about the American working for wages or salary who are surveyed and studied to the last decimal point. We know, for instance, that the average firefighter makes $362.00 a week and that the average man entering the employed workforce at 16 will work for 38.5 years. There are periodic massive studies of worker dissatisfaction—the study of which *Newsweek* once said had become an industry unto itself.

The next two chapters are an attempt to distinguish the self-employed from the rest of the herd, starting with a survey of a number of resourceful and very diverse people so employed.

3

PROJECT WATERCOOLER

The Self-Employed
State of Mind

He must fight *The Organization. Not stupidly, or selfishly, for the defects of individual self-regard are no more to be venerated than the defects of co-operation. But fight he must, for the demands for his surrender are constant and powerful...*

—William H. Whyte, Jr.
The Organization Man

The survey was set up like a chain letter in that I started with a few names of self-employed people and from them got the names of other independents and from them still more. The idea simply was to get in touch with at least 100 diversely self-employed people and question them, by mail, phone and in person, about their state of work. I was interested in a number of things ranging from why they did it to the extent to which they were using computers and other pieces of electronic gear.

Put another way, I was looking for the same kind of information that employed people pass around the watercooler. Living as I do, close to Washington, D.C., I felt compelled to give this effort a spiffy code name and was naturally attracted to *"Project Watercooler."*

From the outset I knew that this would not be a scientific survey yielding me a pile of percentages and correlations, but rather a number of insights from a motley crew of widely dispersed self-employed Americans. I sent out some 400 letters and questionnaires over a period of about a year and got back almost half of them. The questionnaires were informal and designed for discussion rather than simple yes and no answers. Some people just used the questionnaire as an outline and ended up writing me long letters touching on the points that interested me.

By any measure it was a chain letter that worked. Not only did I get leads from other self-employed but the magazine *In Business* and several newsletters carried notice of my project and I was able to get new leads this way. An article I wrote in *Creative Living* magazine on the subject of self-employment netted me letters from people whom I promptly enlisted.

When it was all done, I ended up with a bulging file of letters, notes and completed questionnaires and a lot of new insight into what goes into being self-employed. Many had put a number of hours into their answers for which I thank them here and by name in the acknowledgments at the end of the book.

They had come from all over and represented just about all of the major self-employed professions including carpenters, writers, designers, store owners, consultants, photographers, craftspeople, accountants, tutors, printers, restaurant-owners, psychotherapists, engineers and mechanics. I also netted one freelance marine biologist, a woman whose writing specialty had been hard-core pornography, and one full-time astrologer. Geographically, they ranged from the owner of a weekly newspaper in Stonington, Maine, to a jeweler in Hilo, Hawaii. In all, people in 37 states participated.

There were several who had more than one independent career going at the same time and a few that ranged widely within their field—such as the professional classical musician whose concerts have been played in places ranging from restaurants to a traveling cocktail party in the back of a Winnebago.

Significantly, some of the people clustered around my watercooler were in fields which were either unheard of or in the "lost arts" category not that long ago. There were, for example, two full-time freelance calligraphers and one information broker in the survey. Imagine telling your high school guidance counselor in 1968 that you were going to make your living in the late 20th century as a calligrapher—an art that had gone through its last revival in the 1880s. Information brokers, or freelance research librarians, weren't even heard of in 1968.

Because of the way in which this was set up, I realize that the people who ended up in my dragnet tended to be those who would be most content and at ease with their status, while those who were dissatisfied might be inclined to pass on the prospect of answering a lot of questions. To compensate for this, I tried to get people to dwell on the negative aspects of self-employment through a series of leading questions. I also strongly suspect that at least a few of the people whom

I wrote to but chose not to enlist were people who were *bona fide* members of the underground economy, so the survey is free of tax outlaws.

In general, the vast majority of the people polled were unincorporated and working alone. There were a handful of mom and pop operations, and a few were individuals who had incorporated for tax reasons. Only a smattering employed others, most of these being people with retail shops. The people responding were almost equally divided between men and women. The number of years people had been self-employed ranged from one to 49 and the ages at which they had started ranged from two who had started at 17 (a freelance photographer and an independent insurance salesman) to a man who began at 66. The average person I surveyed had started between the ages of 31 and 32 and had been self-employed for a little less than nine years. The age of the people who answered the questions averaged a few months short of 40.

Because I felt it was none of my business, I did not ask people about how much income they made, but it was clear from other answers that these were people who for the most tended to make moderate amounts of money, having long ago traded off the prospect of high income for such things as independence, foreign travel, time with the family and, above all, being able to work in a field they loved. If there was one strong undercurrent at work in people's responses it was a passion for what they were doing.

There were, however, extreees. Several had obviously made lots of money. Several had run more than one independent business. One man who was faced with a major promotion in a *Fortune* 500 company realized that the corporate ladder was not for him, so he quit, traveled around Europe and the United States for a year and went back home to Nebraska to start two successful small businesses—a photography studio and a pizza restaurant. Several confidently reported that their first million was within sight.

A few lived near or below the poverty line. One independent writer/researcher has remained self-employed primarily because of his ability to find house-sitting assignments (and by not being too proud to sleep in his car between assignments) and to locate "alternative sources" of food. Writing about this, he has revealed some of his secrets including wild foods free for the gathering and merchants who give him what they normally throw away, blemished peaches and the like. "Material life moved up another peg when I found out that they actually throw away lobster bodies in the fish store. I took some home. Heaven." In order to hold it all together, he has waited on tables, worked as a night watchman and become an auto dentist (filling and painting rust holes which, as his ad points out, "like tooth decay, keep growing until they are filled"). Through it all he has retained a true and optimistic sense of entrepreneurial bravado: "I am both a watchman and a corporation president, the peer of the owner of the watchman company. My corporation is in a cardboard carton."

By category, here is what I learned from *Project Watercooler* starting with the discovery of the extent to which self-employment can be ideological and anti-institutional. If nothing else, this survey found out where some of those square pegs ended up: they made their own square holes.

FIERCE INDEPENDENCE

Everyone was asked why they thought the numbers of self-employed had risen so dramatically in recent years. The answers here as in other areas were varied. "The same reason why the divorce rate increased," said a California psychotherapist, "people are less willing to tolerate less than they perceive themselves capable of." She added, "Perhaps, also—on the negative side—increased incidence of narcissism due to child-rearing practices of the 1950s." Others cited such diverse factors as the need or desire of a parent to be available to the children, the jolt of recession, the desire to make more money and the infatuation with the risk of entrepreneurship. Several felt that the desire by many to get out beyond the city and its suburbs had been at play. "There just weren't that many jobs in the county," said one speaking from his own experience, "so we created our own."

But if there was one common thread which ran through most all of the answers it was a deep disregard for the corporate life and its pressures. One cannot understate the extent to which this anti-corporate feeling pervaded the answers. To some it was something simply stated—on the order of "disillusionment with a standard corporate career," or, "to escape the rat race,"—but to others it was something much more specific indicated by this response from Barbara Zimmerman, a New York copyright consultant:

> Let me give you my reason for going into business for myself—perhaps, if others share it, you will have a trend. About ten years ago the firm I worked for fired a 55-year-old man with five children, three in college. This man had tripled their business and put them on the map. He was not fired for age or incompetence, but because they had decided to sell the firm. In order to make a better bottom line for the buyer-to-be, the owners decided the simplest thing would be get rid of one executive with a large salary and let the new owners replace him. They tossed a coin to see who it would be. I was there when they did it. From that moment on I understood that I never wanted anyone to do that to me.

An independent automobile mechanic with his own shop in Maryland cited another type of corporate experience: "Anyone who works for a large company, and I did, cannot help but be struck by how rigid such concerns are. They cannot change with the needs of the market. They tend to frustrate their workers and often their clients. Such businesses train and create the self-employed. They show us their shortcomings and inform us to the size and needs of their client base. I never thought about opening a shop until I saw how badly the work was being done and how unhappy the clients were."

Some were anti-corporate for their own reasons. "My weakest personality trait is that I cannot abide people telling me what to do," said an independent graphic designer from Massachusetts, who also disliked the corporate tendency to turn everyone into a specialist. He now relished the fact that he had a broad range of responsibilities in his one-man shop, unlike in his former incarnation as a specialist in an ad agency. Another person found that she could not adjust to office work where she was unable to see the tangible (or even intangible) results of her work.

Others were very specific in their dislike for the insecurity of standard employment: being subjected to layoffs, firings or forced retirements, having your job automated, being replaced by a younger or better educated worker. A Florida woman now in business with her husband answered, "Because so many large companies made it difficult for older people or people such as my husband who had heart disease." Several people mentioned the "white collar lay-off" as a big factor. "People who had devoted themselves to their corporations found themselves out on the street," said consultant and independent publisher Jeffrey Lant. "From that unenviable position they resolved it would 'never happen again.'"

"Being managed" ranked high as a specific complaint. An independent chemist went on at length over corporate structures top heavy with non-productive MBAs and concluded, "For those who have the work ethic, self-employment is the only way to 'do' rather than be 'done to.'"

Nobody complained that they were overworked or pushed too hard in traditional jobs, but rather expressed the belief that self-employment was invariably more demanding and satisfying. "It's much more satisfying to be self-employed," said a typical respondent. "When I was a 9-to-5er, I was also a clock-watcher; but in all the years since, I've worked much longer days and never minded. This is largely because everything good that accrues from my work is for my own benefit." Some answers let you know that self-employed people were a different breed: "Some people have too much talent to be content working for a large, slow organization."

Yet, along with this kind of deep disregard for the corporate life many people cited their belief that it is an old-fashioned American trait to want to get out from under the boss's thumb and become your own boss. "Americans are basically entrepreneurial," said Bill Casey of Denver. To some, it would seem that self-employment was a clear representation of established values while corporate values represented something new, depersonalizing and corrupt. "More people were really traditionalists," said an independent salesman from Atlanta, "and wanted to work hard and control their own lives." Again and again, people unflinchingly referred to the American Dream and its continuing power to motivate. A sizable number of people saw the roots of their corporate feeling in events: the failure of the Penn Central, Watergate, the war in Vietnam and, as one woman put it, "...numerous disappointments from our corporate culture [which] have taught us that big is not necessarily beautiful."

Although the question had to do with the population at large, there were many who had to relate it directly to their own cases. These often had to do with opportunities which only existed through self-employment. "My own situation is unique," said cabinetmaker Marsha Vander Heyden, "because I'm a woman in a blue collar trade and I ended up with my own business because no one would hire me." A Texas woman who has been self-employed in both the construction business and photography said, "Especially for women, the opportunities for bright, entrepreneurial types are better on the outside of the establishment."

A Kansas City couple, Dick Brown and Ann Powell-Brown, who had just started their own mom and pop business, put it this way, "We think that there have not been enough jobs. Nor has the quality of jobs available been what the college-educated person expected. Most of us grew up with the idea that getting an education meant you would have 'the world by the tail' as an adult. Since then college-educated people have discovered that if they could get a job at all it was likely to be as a vacuum cleaner salesman. They have had to become somewhat creative and develop their own way to make money."

At least one man, Michael Smith, who runs his own lawn maintenance and landscaping business in El Centro, California, had a Vietnam veteran's perspective on why the experts missed the upturn in self-employment: "Our belief is that there was a war going on and the people who should have been questioned and never were, were off fighting that war. When they returned it was them that started their small businesses. Those that weren't fighting in the war were in college to get a degree only to graduate and enter into an already established firm or corporation."

Age was a factor for some people. Halbert F. Speer, who has been a freelance publishing consultant for the last eight years, said: "I'm 65 years old, and no company would consider putting me on their payroll, but as an (outside) consultant, I'm welcome."

ELECTRONIC EVOLUTION

If there was a surprise in all of this, it was that of the first 120 people interviewed *nobody* even mentioned computers or new technology as a major factor in attracting people into self-employment even though many had been helped by such equipment and a number alluded to the new opportunities created by new technology. From this sampling at least, it would seem that such things are conveniences—miraculous ones to some—that make it easier, but are not the reasons *why* people go off on their own. Much of what is being written about the once and future lure of telecommuting and electronic cottages suggests that it is convenience and cheap circuitry that motivates this kind of independence. The ideology of independence is seldom mentioned; yet, it may be the root of it all.

A separate question asked to what extent the person had been helped by computers, copy machines and phone answering-machines. The phone-answering machine was clearly the most important of the three, with the vast majority calling it essential. For a number of people the answering machine was an instrument to be used *while* they were near the phone as a means of screening and deferring calls. Copy machines were the second most important and many mentions of computers were phrased in the future tense, as in, "I hope to get a word processor sometime next year." Others reported having just gotten computers. It seems likely that the computer revolution has not yet hit these entrepreneurs but that when it does, the results could be quite spectacular.

A few people, however, were clearly wiring their electronic cottages. A Virginia advertising writer, Marybeth Highton, said, "I recently acquired a home computer, software for word processing, a printer, a modem, communicating software, and subscriptions to online data bases such as The Source. I run my business from a home office and comfortably support a household of four with it. When I saw the way the wind was blowing, I started taking college courses in data processing and microcomputer use. I'm now teaching myself BASIC programming language (slowly). My hope is to create a unique commercial-writing niche in the new technology fields. I envision it including the development of advertising concepts and copy for computer-related industries and possibly the writing of software documentation as well as videotex copy of various types." In contrast, a weaver from Michigan bragged that none of this was for her and she didn't have a phone as she lived out beyond the end of the lines.

On the other hand, if there was a surprise it was the extent to which there was an acknowledgment of the countercultural influences of the 60s and the environmental concerns of the 70s as forces leading to self-employment. "Many of our friends are 'children of the 60s,' still influenced by the ideas of that era. Even though those people are 'establishment' by the standards of the 60s, they still don't really want to be part of a corporate structure," was a typical and oft-stated explanation.

Finally, there was the matter of beating Uncle Sam. Some brought this up with more than a hint of bitterness. Taxpayers, irked by the fact that others had been drawn into self-employment by the realization that the Internal Revenue Service was probably not going to catch them, were upset. A writer in California reported, "I know I have found in my own work that there is a significant underground economy and many of these people opt for self-employment as it permits them more easily to 'go off the books.' I know one former school teacher who is making three times what she made teaching for the public schools, and she is continually booked up. I understand that to get her as a tutor, parents get on a waiting list and pray that she will be available in time for their children. With this kind of economic leverage, the alleged 'loss' of benefits that she would have gotten from the school district is, of course, insignificant."

REWARDS

A revealing set of answers was given to the question "What are the particular rewards you've gotten from being self-employed?" I felt these were revealing because so many of them stressed the person's ability to serve others—to do some good, to give a customer good service or create a good product. "The biggest reward," said one man, "is being able to go to bed at night knowing that I have always done my best to help my clients and customers." Another put it this way: "I get tremendous satisfaction from doing good jobs and knowing that other people can easily recognize when I've done a good job."

Another common theme was the straightforward simplicity and completeness of it all: finding work, getting paid for it and going out and buying groceries with the money without a lot of middlemen getting into the act. "My life is greatly simplified in a special way in that I only deal with those things that are significant," said a woman with her own farm, "I rarely deal with individuals I can't stand." A therapist enjoyed the "sense of reality and sanity in being paid directly by the client I serve, who leaves if he or she is not satisfied..."

With this simplicity and directness comes a level of involvement explained by a freelance advertising writer: "A paycheck that's assured, week in and week out, can lull me into a sense of complacency that shows up in my writing. Employed by one ad agency, with a steady income, I can say 'Ah, that's good enough' about a piece of copy that might need just one more rewrite to make it truly 'good enough.' Self-employed, I don't do that. I polish and revise my work until each piece of it is worth sending a bill out for. Moreover, I find myself intensely appreciative of my clients...grateful that they call me...eager to keep them pleased...sympathetic to their problems...attuned to their needs...in a way I am not as their employee."

Some enjoyed the continued risk of it. "This might seem like a strange thing to consider a 'reward,' but I've found self-employment to have the same kind of high that one might have walking along a beautiful mountain path from which one could slip and fall at any moment," was the way a woman who had been self-employed for eight years put it.

A number of people mentioned their ability to be with their families as a prime reward. A highly successful writer lists as the most important reward of self-employment the time he was able to spend with his two sons when they most needed it. "Their first years, I was Washington correspondent for a major newspaper, and during the 1968 election year I was away from home perhaps three-fourths of the time. The next years I was at home when they came in from school; we played ball together, I ran both Cub Scout and Indian Guide groups; we enjoyed some intense experiences that gave us a permanent bond." A Michigan woman put it in these terms: "People have been pushed too far and have come full circle back to the home. From my experience if you are satisfied with your...life, you don't need to go to an office everyday to work."

Success and recognition were rewards that had accrued to some. At the top of a list of rewards listed by a New York book designer: "The knowledge that you have been successful, that you have made it." She then listed money, recognition and the respect of colleagues and competitors and ends with the line "I have become an adult in my field." Another took delight in that he declared himself an expert in his field and has since been regarded as one.

And a few actually claimed that they had, in fact, been able to live out their fondest dreams. A musician and music teacher from Ohio is able to play his guitar for four or five hours a day and occasionally travel through Europe—exactly what he had dreamed of being able to do when he was a kid. A Long Island consultant picks clients in places he enjoys, such as Santa Fe, so he can spend time in those places, and another consultant finds that she can prospect for new clients on ski trips.

Freedom was tremendously important as was the ability to have some control over one's life—"...the wonderful sense of self-control," as one person put it. Not having limits imposed by others was also important, driving one man to quit his job at 55 because he was no longer being allowed to develop new abilities. In all of this, the words that people kept coming back to were freedom, control and independence. James P. Clark, self-employed since December 1945 as a New Jersey manufacturer's representative, looked back on a number of financial and personal rewards but then concluded, "Independence, I suppose, is really the great reward: Captain of my soul."

Some of the answers were refreshingly specific. My favorite discussion of rewards was from Hank Nuwer, a writer in South Carolina: "I'm far from old at age 36. I play baseball, lift weights and smile a lot. I've lived ten lives as a freelancer. I've gotten an opportunity to play first base for a day with the Montreal Expos' organization, herd sheep in Nevada with a Basque herder, stay with a female herder in Idaho, travel with a latter day bounty hunter, and meet all sorts of fascinating people. While those I graduated from college with look burned out, I'm as enthusiastic and as charged about life as I was at twenty. Besides, I'm my own man. No one owns me. You don't have to lick some ass that you'd just as soon be tattooing your boot against!"

Several people listed among their rewards the fact that they had created an occupation and because of that received a modicum of fame. Katherine Ackerman, a pioneering information broker, was justifiably thrilled when she was featured in *Forbes* magazine, and Charisma Clay of Philadelphia, who runs an escort service (including escorts for senior citizens), has experienced "lots of local fame" and sent along a long list of newspaper articles and radio and television interviews.

All of this is not to say that money was not a consideration. "I make more money in one hour than I could working manual labor for a week," said a photographer, and a self-publisher put it all simply, "I have the time and money to do anything I want."

REGRETS

Everyone was asked, "Have you ever regretted the move to become self-employed? If so, when and why?" In a sense, it was a bad question because so many—a clear majority—answered with a curt "no," "never" or "hell, no." In fact, at one point five questionnaires in a row were returned with a simple no. Here are some of the other answers.

"I'm having pangs of regret right now that I'm making so much income that I screwed myself out of a divorce settlement from my husband. But no, not about the self-employment part."
—Retail store owner, St. Louis

"Only when I'm scared and afraid I won't make a living and will end up as a bag lady."
—Weaver and teacher, Maryland

"Yes, everytime I try to go to sleep at night. No, everytime I get up in the morning."
—Manufacturer's rep, Pennsylvania

"My husband died in July, 1983. I could not afford to take time off to recuperate emotionally and had to face immediate legal and financial mountains."
—Writer, Virginia

"No—actually I average several job offers each year. My self-employment has made me a superior person in that I am able to handle most problems in stride and with confidence (though I do have my moments). I am really a better well-rounded individual."
—Marketing consultant, Maryland

"Yes, two years after I started I wrote editorials people didn't like and I was shunned for a while by some people. It made me doubt some of my principles—social disapproval is a strong force—but I decided I was right and they were wrong."
—Small-town newspaper owner, Maine

"I never have regretted it. Once, for a space of five months, I gave it up to work for one firm, though under especially liberal terms that included naming my hours and working from home. Even though that felt like, looked like, seemed like self-employment, it wasn't. I missed the control I had over every aspect of my life and work, and I returned to freelancing."
—Advertising copywriter, Virginia

"Never. Just sorry I didn't start ten years sooner, in order to develop a much larger business..."
—Industrial plating business owner, Tennessee

"Occasionally, when I see peers who have been with corporations for ten years or so and make incredible amounts of money, but of course I realize I've made trade offs."
—Contractor, Virginia

"Only when I think of making more money. But I've always been able to fight it down and stay as I am—satisfied and responsible for my own acts."
—Architect, New Jersey

"Sure. Being self-employed isn't a cake walk. You are it. Responsible for everything. Payroll taxes, filing forms on time, paying the bills, satisfying clients. Most become workaholics, causing family stress. You lose a client, start worrying about the phone not ringing, rejection. Is it worth it? You bet."
—Writer and lecturer, Virginia

"Every month when the rent is due. Not many people can freelance, but for those who do the freelance jitters remain."
—Freelance photographer, New York

Remarkably, the general glibness and spirit of this sampling of answers were reflected throughout. If there were deep regrets, they had apparently been repressed long ago or were not for public consumption. The closest that any of the answers came to true regrets were from a woman who "sometimes" misses the interaction she had with others when she was on the staff of a large publishing company, a man who listed "many regrets" (insecurity, nagging self-doubt, lack of social stimulation, etc.) but who also listed a particularly long list of rewards, and one man who after three years was exhausted, drained and still waiting for profits.

Several women and one male inventor regretted the fact that they were not taken as seriously as they would be if they were working for a corporation. Penelope Comfort Starr, who designs architectural stained glass, had this to say: "A self-employed artist, especially a married female self-employed artist, is pretty low on the status pole. I got lots of attention when I was an employee of a national management consulting firm, flying all over the US to work on jobs. Now, many, maybe most, of the people I know casually assume that my work in glass is something I do part time, or in my garage and are astonished when they come see my studio or read my resume. They just don't take it seriously."

COMPLAINTS

Another question I asked was, "Do you have any specific complaints about being self-employed—things like the Federal self-employment tax, difficulty in getting health insurance, etc.?" Again, what was striking about these answers to an admittedly leading question was the lack of negativism. Many said none, while others simply listed the predictable litany of being overtaxed and underinsured. Clearly, the self-employment tax led in terms of specific gripes. "The self-employment tax is murder," said a California writer, "especially with the whole system on the brink of bankruptcy." The fact that this was a "double-tax" was mentioned by a number of people. An artist from North Carolina said what others implied: "The Social Security system is a mess! I'm paying far too much for benefits I'm sure I'll never see."

The second biggest complaint had to do with the difficulty or inability to get health insurance. A disabled veteran was among those who complained about the fact that companies like Blue Cross would not insure him—although he was fortunate in that he was finally able to get insurance through his wife's policy. Another man who had been self-employed for 22 years was only able to afford health insurance about half of that time. Others complained about disability insurance.

A few listed local taxes as especially irksome. "The New York City unincorporated income tax amounts to double taxation," said a freelance editor. Several felt that the process of paying taxes was too complicated. "I'm glad to live in a country where I have the privilege of paying taxes," said a Seattle man. "I just wish they would make it easier for me to give them my money."

Several people mentioned other regulatory problems and the attendant paperwork, and there were harsh words for licensing boards and regulations. "California state licensing requirements almost state that you have to be in businesses or doing the business that you are trying to be licensed for before you are accepted for the licensing examination," said one man, adding, "Filling out the forms is harder than the test."

A few complaints of this nature came from a woman selling mail-order crafts: "I have been unable to locate the answer to one question. When and if I sell stuffed items wholesale across the country, do I need a license (stuffing license) for each state I sell to? I have called every organization I can think of (consumer protection, SBA, etc.) and was always referred to someone else. I am still searching for the answer."

More than a few pointed to the difficulty in getting paid and a photographer complained about the inability which prospective employers have "...understanding that the self-employed create their own 'benefits' through their day rates."

One man mentioned his inability to get credit cards and another said he had had an initial problem getting bank loans. Financing to several was something you could get only after you no longer needed it. An antique dealer from Connecticut puckishly brought up the issue of the brain depletion allowance: "It is my contention that as a self-employed person, as I get older, my abilities decline; therefore, throughout my business lifetime, I should be able to depreciate myself on my income tax."

A psychotherapist complained about vacations: "Vacations *feel* like they cost twice as much because I lose pay as well as paying usual expenses, and my practice decreases if I'm gone more than a week." A retailer's complaint: "There are things I need to know about (tax laws changing or whatever) that I don't know about and I don't know I don't know about."

Still trying to get complaints, I used another part of my questionnaire to ask about *external* problems which have been encountered along the way. Once again, many people simply stated that there had been none. Several reported red tape in getting business permits and/or an official OK to work at home. An independent realtor in Hawaii got cleared to work at home but was prohibited from putting up a sign or advertising his house as a place of business. The sign problem was repeated by a Texas man.

Some admitted that they were in violation of local laws and one man reported that he was not only in violation of local zoning but also violating the rules of his apartment building. In all, at least a score of those surveyed mentioned that they were or had been working in violation of some prohibition and worried about being turned in by a disapproving neighbor, while others hinted that they might be illegal in that they complained of antiquated zoning rules. A "typical" illegal, a Californian, wrote, "Running a business out of our home in this area is not legal. We get around it by using a P.O. box and not notifying our local government. I am confiding in you and trust you will not print this information with our names or notify our local government." Several were not sure if they were or were not illegal, but had wisely decided not to ask and to retain "a low profile." A Massachusetts woman was told that she needed a zoning change to work at home and that it would cost $100 to have a hearing on such a change. Deeming all of this unreasonable, she ignored the whole thing and was not bothered.

However, of all these external issues the one mentioned most often was establishing credit and/or getting credit cards. Several women attributed this problem to their being women, but the problem seemed to be just as common among men. An independent contractor who'd been making a living on his own for ten years reported that he'd just been turned down for a department store credit card. A woman from Wisconsin put it this way: "I am unable to establish credit because either (1) I am self-employed, (2) I am an artist, (3) I am a self-employed artist." Several people reported that they had never bothered to tell those who issued them credit cards when they were employed that they were now self-employed.

WORKING HOURS

There was great variety in the number of hours that people worked, but the tendency was to a heavy workload averaging a little more than 50 hours a week. A number worked at workaholic paces of 60 or more hours a week, a few relished the fact that they could make a living at 25 hours a week with plenty of time to play, but most said that they could get it all done by working an average of 38 to 42 hours a week. Several put great emphasis on their freedom not to work, such as a computer systems designer who only worked 20 hours a week and was able to brag, "I schedule my work around recreational activities, not the other way around." The extremes were an architect who said he averaged 100 hours of work a week (although he did take six weeks of vacation) and a marine biologist who, after ten years of self-employment, was able to make a living working a mere ten hours a week (he also took six weeks of vacation).

Flexibility in hours was the norm with only a few people saying that they were on a rigid daily schedule. A number pointed out that their work patterns changed throughout the course of the year. In this category was an importer from Oregon who hardly worked at all during her slow season around Christmas but adopted a rigid and busy schedule during the periods in the year when she was attending trade shows. Several people chose to work afternoons and evenings, reserving their mornings for things like gardening or swimming. A number reported that they broke from work when the kids came home from school. One woman was an admitted "early, early morning person" and typically worked from 5:00 A.M. to noon.

There were also those who seasonally adjusted their work. A New York writer/editor/agent typically works from 7:00 A.M. to 11:00 P.M. in the cold months, but, "In the summer months...and in the springtime, there is too much temptation, and I work shorter hours, knocking off to play stickball with the local kids, in the middle of the afternoon, or to work in my tiny garden, or just sit outside and read."

The vast majority took only two or three weeks vacation a year and the average fell between two and three weeks. A few treated themselves to six to eight weeks and there were more than a few who didn't take any vacation. A freelance photojournalist who took no vacation pointed out, however, that he was constantly traveling, which presumably made up for his need to vacation in the normal sense of the word.

Some people, however, reported that they had so blurred the distinction between work and play that they didn't know which was which anymore.

WORKPLACE

Most of the people contacted work at home full time or part of the time. The dislike of commuting was universal and many of those with offices or shops outside the home were close enough to the office to be able to walk to work and amble home for lunch. A few "commuted" to an outbuilding on their property such as a garage which had been converted into a studio or office. Those who drove to a place of business told of being able to drive in the direction where there was the least traffic. Avoiding the traditional commute was seen as a way of avoiding stress—"I don't need two drinks to unwind from rush hour anymore and I'm not as crabby as I used to be," said one former commuter—and picking up valuable time—"I 'save' at least a week's work in portal to portal time, and probably much more," commented another.

Those who worked at home generally loved the arrangement but admitted occasional problems: friends or clients who dropped in during working hours, the ongoing battle for workspace with other members of the family; and, as one woman put it, "At times I dislike working at home because it constantly reminds me of all the various things I should be doing. It, therefore, makes it more difficult to relax at home since almost anywhere I look I see my business papers, equipment or merchandise." One person faced with this problem ended up leasing an office and another, who enjoyed working at home, opened an office in a nearby office building in part because it "shows clients that you are a legit business rather than a freelancer who's easily abused." One went "mildly stir crazy" at home and signed a lease on an office so that he could participate in the excitement and energy of the downtown workday. Several admitted to occasional periods when they felt isolated or lonesome.

Elizabeth Grindle, a Floridian accountant whose specialty is taxes, was forced to leave her home office: "When I worked at home clients felt free to drop by unannounced at any hour of the day or night. I even had clients call at midnight to ask about their tax returns...This drove me crazy, because the clients that were considerate enough not to call during the middle of the night would call at 6:30 or 7:00 in the morning. In April, I found it impossible to get eight hours of uninterrupted sleep."

One man recalled the drawback of working at home in the suburbs: "I was the available person when a neighbor or a school group needed a daytime chore performed because, 'you don't work.' I did PTA and other stuff cheerfully; in fact, my daytime freedom enabled me to become a minor power in county zoning politics. But the view that I was 'unemployed' was sometimes grating in view of the fact that I made up for the volunteer hours by working late at night." Despite this, the man is still working at home. Others mentioned the fact that it was difficult getting their friends to understand that just because they were at home didn't mean they welcomed impromptu visits. There were times, some said, when the working and home worlds collided. "Don't invite clients to a home office that isn't soundproofed," said a consultant. "During one such visit, my children's 17 guinea pigs started squealing."

Significantly, however, none listed their children as a problem (although one did note that he was looking forward to the day that his nine-month-old did not need to be changed as often), but a number reported that it was an advantage to be around the kids and be there when they needed them. A few people made the obvious point that one's sex life improves when working at home and the devoted pet lovers pointed out that they got a real lift from being around their animals. "My cats are spoiled rotten," wrote one man. One man said that working at home allowed him to take care of an elderly and disabled parent.

A few described their situation as ideal. A Nebraska man said, "My home office is great. I built it as a new office attached onto my house. There is a separate entry for business appointments, yet it is accessible through the house. I have a beautiful view of the lake, trees and birds. I can watch my three-year-old daughter grow and am available when my wife is away from home: something I missed with my older children."

PERSONAL CHARACTERISTICS

The question: "What personal characteristics do you think have been most useful to you in establishing your self-employed career?"

Discipline, determination and the ability to self-start were the traits mentioned most often. Next came self-confidence and the ability to take risk. Washington, D.C.-based writer Mike Whalen had this to say about risk taking: "Most of my employed friends envy me but think I'm highly imprudent in not providing for my old age. I tell them that by the time I'm old I'll either be rich, dead or used to living on nothing."

These traits were followed closely by a cluster of characteristics having to do with communicating with others both in conversation and via the written word. A number reported their ability to speak a foreign language as a special advantage in their work. A typical answer was this one from a mechanic: "I am a verbal person. I can easily make myself understood by a wide range of people. In any small shop or business much of your time, too much really, is spent in explaining and requesting. In speaking to my clients I try to give them enough information to involve them in decisions. In a sense I educate them and I think I do this well."

Some mentioned high personal standards as their competitive edge and one man simply held that such high standards were all that he had to offer, but that was enough. Another said it was a blend of personal integrity and a good sense of humor. A few mentioned arrogance—as opposed to self-confidence—and a few others listed such things as hunger and big mortgages.

Persistence ranked high and was expressed in various ways including the ability to work through minor illnesses and ailments. "In six years," said one man, "I haven't taken a single day of sick leave. It's not because I'm particularly healthy. It's just because if I don't show up, it doesn't get done."

Some of the answers given by women were especially interesting. A woman from California said, "Growing up as a tomboy. Learning how to sail at 14 and having my own boat at 15. (My dad refused the normal horse.) Early independence and feeling of being able to take care of myself. Willingness to follow my intuition as well as intellect." A woman from Washington, D.C. attributed part of her success to "an ex-husband who didn't want me to go out to work full-time—so I had to develop my own inner life and discipline."

Perhaps the most unusual answer came from a California architect who had this to say about himself: "When I was little I used to be good at imitating Charlie Chaplin and Laurel and Hardy. Then, when I grew older, I suppose I decided not to want to imitate anymore, but to become as unique and creative as my heroes, but I never lost that child in me."

A Colorado man said that his most useful characteristic has been his "unsuitability for employment."

GETTING STARTED

I was not only interested in hearing how people started their freelance careers, but also whether or not they had a "safety net" of some sort (a long-term contract, a promise of getting your old job back whenever you wanted it, or whatever.)

The vast majority started cold rather than easing into it by way of a part-time avocation or moonlighting. Some bragged about going out without a net, pointing out, as a Virginia man did, "that the real incentives come only without such a net." All but two had been fully employed or working as a housewife when they started. Some just woke up one morning and finally took the plunge and others had something happen to them. "The company that I was working for went bankrupt." "I was working for someone that I could simply just not get along with." "The company I was working for was sold and the only way to keep my old job was to move to New York City." "Started cold after the magazine I started was sold by the company I worked for."

One net which several people used was the promise that they could have their old job back. Several had arranged long-term retainers, three had loans from members of their families and one man had saved enough from a previous job to keep him going for several years. A small handful had employed spouses who were the net for the first few years.

GROUPS AND ORGANIZATIONS

Everyone was asked to list the organizations which had been helpful to them in their self-employment. Just about half listed none and those that did list groups tended to list professional groups that one might expect, such as the American Institute of Architects, the American Society of Magazine Photographers, the Poetry Society of America and the American Management Association. People who lived in smaller towns mentioned service groups, like Rotary, as good places to meet new clients. Only one person mentioned a group that served large numbers of self-employed from many professional areas, the Small Business Service Bureau, and four had been helped by the Small Business Administration's SCORE, for Service Corps of Retired Executives, a program in which experienced business veterans counsel newcomers on a voluntary basis.

The people who had used SCORE were generous in their praise of it. Louise Borquez, who with her daughter operates a water delivery service called Desert Roadrunner's in 29 Palms, California, said: "They pulled us out of a hole when we almost went under. They

showed us where the mistakes were and how we could cure them and
set us on the road to recovery."

A good third of the people said that they relied on informal network
arrangements with others working in the same area rather than formal
organizations (although the language used to describe this ranged from
formal network descriptions to talk of having a couple of beers once a
week with others in the same business). One resourceful woman with a
paper and party supply business could not find a group of people in
the same business so she founded one.

Two people mentioned the fact that they planned to use their
computers to communicate with others in their field with the aid of
computer services like The Source.

Clearly, however, this was not a group of compulsive joiners and the
tendency was to "hack it alone" or rely on a select few groups.

2000 YEARS WORTH OF GOOD ADVICE

Although the idea behind *Project Watercooler* was not to solicit "how
to" information, it did present an ideal opportunity to find out the
lessons others had learned. In two separate sections of the
questionnaire I asked for advice on becoming self-employed. One
question asked, "If a close friend, son or daughter was going to strike
out on their own in a self-employed career, what key piece of advice
would you pass along?" The second asked for more mundane tips.

As there was something on the order of 2,000 years worth of self-
employed experience represented by those who had enlisted in *Project
Watercooler*, it would have been insane not to pick up a few lessons.
From a list of hundreds of items—a barrage of them, far more than I
had anticipated—some 55 major points emerged as the most
important, with many of them repeated again and again. I have
distilled them into the following communal list, stating them as if they
were given by one person. In no special order, they are:

1. Make sure you pick a field that you really love. It's tough enough
    working for someone else at a job you don't care for, but to work
    for yourself at something you don't care for is impossible. Sign
    maker Mark Zilliox says you've got to decide if you just want to
    make money or you want to "make a living." If you want to make a
    living, you're on the right track.

2. Don't allow well-meaning friends to pressure you into thinking you
    are now insecure and that the only form of job security comes with
    a conventional 9-to-5 job. Think of the woman in our survey
    whose self-employment "safety net" was her husband's full-time

job. He lost his job nine months later and the wife's business supported the family for the eight months he looked for a new job.

3. Ignore all those statistics which tell you that 95% of all new businesses fail in the first eight years. Not only are these "statistics" riddled with wildly wrong assumptions and false failure rates (some count people who apply for licenses but never actually go into business as failed businesses) but they don't apply to you. Dwelling on these statistics is like staying up to study divorce rates on your wedding night. One woman put it this way: "In matters of success and failure...above all don't listen to anyone who is not self-employed."

4. From the very beginning you must think of yourself as a business, which is sometimes hard for artists and artisans to do. "It is amazing," said an independent designer, "how even the most unpretentious small endeavor becomes a 'business'! Alas, most of us are not very inclined to manage a business, or even want to do it. However, we are forced to become our own business managers and success or failure may come to depend on our talent in this area."

5. Learn your business on somebody else's time. Stay with a regular job to learn all you can. Stay with it as long as you have to.

6. Before you hang out your own shingle, learn about the special taxes, licenses and regulations that you will have to abide by. A few hours on the phone and in the library checking these things out can save much grief down the line.

7. Learn the legitimate tax breaks which accrue to you. As basic as this sounds, many of us have been burned badly because we overpaid taxes in the first few years.

8. Pay your taxes on time, report all income and prepare your tax forms carefully. This is not only an ethical matter but a practical one as well because you don't want to invite tax troubles which can eat up large amounts of time. The odds of a tax audit are much greater if you are self-employed.

9. No matter what your age, set up your retirement funds (Keogh and IRA) as soon as possible. This is the major break you're going to get from Uncle Sam and you're nuts if you don't take advantage of it.

10. Hire the best accountant you can get and ask every question you can think of: for instance, "Is it more advantageous to lease a car for business or purchase one?" Once this has been done, make sure that you understand everything that is going on. Don't ever get too far away from your books. One woman advises other self-employed people to audit themselves after a year or two—"You'll be surprised at how good you'll feel knowing

everything is all straight."

11. Double or triple the estimates of time and money it will take you to get off the ground.

12. As far as possible, prepare yourself for the inevitable periods when you will be lonely. One woman discovered, "You may not realize how much you are psychically 'fed' by co-workers until you break away from it." (One self-boss reports that he learned to talk with himself: "These conversations have developed into arguments. What disturbs me is that I am losing the arguments.")

13. Realize, too, that there will be failures which you cannot lay at anyone else's feet or blame on "the system." A California woman advises that you've got to learn to love the battle for the battle itself and not just the prize you get for winning.

14. Don't be *too* cautious about starting: they don't execute you for going broke or bankrupt. We all know someone who, for years, has been talking about going off on their own when the *time* is ripe. A man who did it by going off on his own as a business consultant said, "The thing that I also learned is that unless one takes a chance, nothing is ever accomplished—now my mother-in-law figured that anyone with kids ages one and four and a mortgage should not really take too many chances—but that is just the problem with our society (and no criticism of my mother-in-law). We are all too afraid to take a chance to strike out, to create something from the start, and to actually be responsible for our actions or inactions."

15. Don't try to do *everything* yourself—get help and advice.

16. Keep track of your "wins"; repress your worst "losses." Moderate it all with humor.

17. Don't forget to look back from time to time to see how far you've come. Where were you six months ago?

18. Allow yourself plenty of time to dream about where you're going, but stay as realistic as possible.

19. Don't count your hours, especially when you are starting because there will be many of them for which you will not be paid. For the first two years all sorts of problems will crop up that you didn't expect and they will all take time to resolve. You should prepare other members of your family for this. Strive for normal hours—40 hours or thereabouts—by the end of the second year and memorize Arthur Lind's law: "Overtime is for honest-to-God emergencies." Lind, a Portland, Oregon, man who gives small business seminars, has come up with a series of rules of thumb for running your own business including this set of "figures":

Normally: 41 hours per week = 39 hours of productivity
45 hours per week = 35 hours of productivity
50 hours per week = 30 hours of productivity
80 hours per week = 0 hours of productivity

Statistics prove that 72% of accidents occur during overtime. It is also true that overtime accounts for:

87% of all Stupid Decisions
92% of all Unnecessary Conflict
101% of all Unwise Sexual Advances

20. Don't keep what you are doing a secret. Let everybody you know in on it. It is remarkable how much work will come your way, both directly and indirectly, because of friends and acquaintances. Contact people in allied areas and let them know you are in business. Tell your dentist, printer and dry cleaner. Try to spare a moment to talk with anyone who is interested in what you are doing. "Some of the most unlikely characters you can imagine end up as your best clients," said an independent accountant. An Oregon woman put it this way: "Get your face and name *out there* for people to see and remember...and pass along. Give public speeches."

21. Do nothing that will limit your vision of what is possible. Think internationally, for instance, if that is appropriate to what you are doing.

22. To the extent possible, surround yourself with people who will support you in your desire to be self-employed and not keep pushing you toward the "security" of a real job. Make sure your kids understand what's going on and, to quote one of the partners in a Texas mom and pop electronics firm, "With small children, giving them jobs they can do in the business keeps them close to you...and teaches them self-reliance which should help when they are out on their own."

23. Do everything you can to develop the habits of self-discipline. Your success may be directly proportional to the amount of self-discipline you exercise.

24. Don't expect anything to be an overnight success. If you think in these terms you are headed for disaster. One man said, "Develop a steady, conservative source of income in your business. Chasing after the big deals without this will kill you."

25. Strive for simplicity, especially when it comes to such things as record keeping and filing. Set up a simple, efficient system for

dealing with correspondence and bills. Don't get buried in paper and, as basic as it sounds, don't defer your own billing. (Several people reported that the biggest problem they ran into the first few years was falling behind in and then fouling up their billing systems.) Once you have set up systems for dealing with these things, strive to make them more efficient.

26. Force yourself to become a fanatical collector of receipts and registrar of expenses. Write everything down, especially the names of people you have spoken to. At the least, you will need a good daybook to tell you where you were, whom you saw and what you spent. "Your memory," said one person, "is your most unreliable employee."

27. Don't become an obsessive planner. Figure that, to some degree, one thing will lead to another. Flexibility is one of the things you've got which most organizations don't have; take advantage of it. "My business has moved in five different directions other than I ever imagined it would," said Jim Cameron, a freelance radio reporter and syndicator. "Had I been adamant, unwilling to recognize opportunities and lacked the flexibility to pursue them, I'd not be where I am today."

28. By the same token, have a clear idea of your goals. When you divert from them, acknowledge the fact to yourself so that you are not surprised when they have to be deferred or dropped. If, for instance, your goal is to become a name in your field, beware of work where your role will be anonymous or buried in a long list of project participants. Also, don't make all your goals long-term ones: a few simple, short-term goals are essential.

29. Don't base your business on a single client or customer. If you must rely on key clients, try to have as many of them as possible. A rule of thumb which has been suggested is that a business should be able to survive the loss of its best customer.

30. The cliched "bottom line" isn't everything; but if you don't pay attention to it, it will get you. No matter what business you are in you must be constantly aware of your financial situation. "Do not confuse symbol with reality," warned management consultant Bill Casey. "Fancy machinery, a decorated office, pretty stationary, and a classy receptionist DO NOT mean that you're in business. Positive cash flow does. Concentrate on the reality. The symbols are secondary."

31. If you are going to work at home, set territorial boundaries immediately and work outside of the family's normal traffic patterns. If you can, work all of this out in advance. Realize that you may be invading someone else's turf. A man who had done just that to his wife explained, "She had married me for better and for worse, but not for lunch." You should have your own room with a door and business-only phone. Be sure that everyone understands what is happening. As a woman with seven children put it: "Make your family respect your work and your workplace. It is not some cute, clever thing you're doing. It's honest work."

32. Learn your own abilities and limits. Don't overload yourself with work—which means learning to say no. Your reputation will be built on quality not quantity.

33. Don't be afraid to let your own personal style emerge. Be sure it fits.

34. As a sole proprietor, you will probably find yourself doing things and having to learn things you never expected. Be prepared to take a course in accounting, do your own promotional mailings, write a fierce dunning letter and any of a thousand other things you hadn't planned on. A self-employed accountant advised: "Don't be afraid to ask for and collect fees on a timely basis. The self-employed person cannot afford to carry accounts receivable for very long...I've found that people will pay when you make it obvious that you expect payment. If you do not make this obvious, they assume they can pay you later (like 90 days!)."

35. Make sure that you find a few solitary moments at the beginning of each workday to plan and put things in perspective. If your work is sedentary, plan some time for exercising—you will, among other things, have more energy.

36. If you are married, make sure your spouse understands what you are up to including *all* the inherent risks. This is doubly important if any joint savings will be on the line. Some people tend to minimize risk based on the mistaken assumption that it will make it seem like a more attractive idea. If you are a mom and pop operation, listen to this mom : "If you're working with your spouse, make a pact not to discuss business the last hour or so before you go to bed and try to have your arguments concerning the business at the business."

37. Set a time limit for the "experiment" and be ready to accept failure if you must. It is much better to bail out—with the option of going out on your own again at a later date—than to hang onto something that isn't going to work. (This advice comes from two people who had initially failed, "gone back to work" and are now successfully self-employed. One of them stressed this point: "...don't hesitate to pull the plug on a failing business that has no chance of succeeding; it doesn't mean *you're* a failure. You'll try again, learning from your mistakes.")

38. Enter as deliberately as possible but don't be afraid of using a part-time job while making the transition. Said one who has done just that, "If you're not sure of yourself, don't have a big bankroll, and can afford to start out part-time, take a part-time job so you don't have to hit the panic button if your business takes a little longer to succeed, and start turning a profit."

39. Take advantage of whatever cushions you can. If your husband or wife has a regular job with group health insurance, see if you can be covered through your spouse's policy. Spousal coverage can save you money and a lot of time.

40. If possible, have some money set aside to help you over the first months. The greatest shock that comes to some newly self-employed people is that just because you have *earned* money does not necessarily mean that you will be *paid*. "Nobody bothered to warn me about this," noted one woman, "I somehow expected someone to drop a pay envelope on my desk like they did when I had a regular job."

41. Line up as much credit as you can before you start. Even something as basic as credit cards can be difficult to obtain for the newly self-employed. Befriend a banker.

42. If you don't have savings to get you through the first months, make sure you have *assured* work lined up. Better yet, *assured work in writing.*

43. Beware of entanglements which can rob you of the very things which brought you to self-employment. One person had a large company willing to buy all of his equipment for his metal-plating business if he would agree to do all of their work. "I had to turn them down as I would be returning to the same position I had previously" as an employee. Similarly, a man with a very small advertising agency was approached by a friendly competitor with the proposal that they merge. "On paper the evidence was overwhelmingly in favor of merger. It meant more income for me, an immediate cash settlement, relief from the financial concerns of running a business, a larger, more competitive company, etc. But still, I couldn't bring myself to even agree to look into the prospect beyond these preliminary steps. I agonized over this hesitancy feeling that I was being selfish and unfair to my family, employees and maybe to myself." He ultimately turned down the merger, realizing that "control over a very significant portion of my life is what will keep me happily—if also hectically—self-employed."

44. Learn how to price your products and your time. You're bound to make mistakes in this area, especially when you are so eager to get going that you underprice yourself. Charge what you are worth, not a cent less. Don't neglect to work your overhead into the fee.

45. Keep your overhead low, but don't scrimp on the essential tools of your profession. Overhead costs tend to creep higher and higher until a slow period comes along to remind you of this.

46. If you can, find a mentor or someone in your line of work who has much more experience. Rely on this person to talk over problems, but share your triumphs with this person as well. Don't think of it as a one-way street: mentors need people to talk with too.

47. From time to time do something dramatic to remind yourself of your freedom: like taking off in the middle of the day to see a movie or a ball game. An occasional four-hour lunch is not a bad idea. Be a good easygoing employer when it comes to such truancy and don't ever reprimand yourself for such behavior or say you should have been working. On the other hand, you must develop the ability to say "no" when someone asks you to goof off when work must be done. Take vacations! One self-employed couple said that the biggest mistake they made during their first five years of self-employment was not taking vacations.

48. Meet occasionally with other self-employed people (preferably in the same racket) to *kvetch*, swap advice, drink beer, talk about world conquest, etc. Keep it informal, but from time to time pick a subject of interest to all of you and discuss it in detail.

49. When given the option of contracting for services or actually hiring people temporarily, opt for the former. The costs and paperwork involved in hiring are tremendous and with employees you come under a whole new collection of government regulations. One exampll, given by a farmer: "Workman's comp. costs are far out of proportion to the type of work and the productivity of the person. I can't hire someone to help with farm chores without risking everything."

50. Don't get big unless you really want to and understand what it implies. Jim Clark, self-employed for 39 years as a manufacturer's representative, testified on this point: "Keep it small. I made the mistake of starting several other businesses all of which were successful, but I overextended myself and got a heart attack at 50. Believe me this will slow you down. Once you get a business going and you know most of the answers and the trials and tribulations, you get a little cocky and figure 'hell, I can start this business and that business.'...Don't fall into this trap. Just keep doing what you can accomplish comfortably and without a lot of stress. The more you take on the more stress you generate. Be careful: keep it simple."

51. Prepare for feast or famine.

52. When it stops being fun, get out.

53. "Pray a lot, be nice, fight like hell to make it, but keep it CLEAN!" advised the mom of a mom and pop business.

54. And finally, as one man expressed it, "Above all, retain the conviction of an Eastern Mystic in ultimate solvency."

4

HOUSE RULES

The Controversial Cottage
and Other Domestic Disturbances

In a way it is the most unlikely of issues—the kind of things that nobody predicted would become a matter for passionate debate—but it has and it promises to be with us for some time to come.

The issue is quite simply whether or not a person has a right to work at home. On one side are those who argue that we should be free to make money in our homes as long as we behave ourselves and don't become a source of a pollution (air, water, noise or traffic). On the other are those who maintain that we must be regulated, as we can be in a factory or an office building, and that in many cases it should be illegal to work at home.

There have always been people who worked at home. Historically, we started working in our home workshops and family farms and later moved into factories and office buildings.

Some of us have dawdled: right into this century the bulk of all Swiss watches and German toys came out of home workshops and there are parts of the third world where cottage industry is the only industry to speak of. In America some of us came out of our homes quicker than others. Garment making, for instance, was primarily a home trade for most of the 19th century. In 1844 a newspaper could report that "every country village within 100 miles of New York became as busy as a beehive with tailors and tailoresses."

At a certain point, not too long ago, it became an American article of faith that except for an occasional artist, we were all destined to go to work in some place other than where we lived. Increasingly, this assumption grew to encompass millions of women coming into the workplace.

A certain idealism was at work as the workplace was spruced up. Industrial parks sprang up in which factories nestled up against a pine grove replete with picnic tables, and the architectural magazines carried articles on new humanitarian workplace design. Never mind what they looked like from the outside, the modern office building was in large part designed to give the people who worked in them a clean, bright place where they would never have to sweat or shiver. Employers laid out hard cash for piped-in music and color-coordinated office equipment.

What's more, for trade unionists and their allies the ancient specter of the exploitive home workshop was in deep retreat. To be sure, horrid examples still cropped up from time to time, especially in urban ghettos and among illegal aliens, graphically showing the extent to which "industrial homework" could be the cover for the vilest forms of worker exploitation ranging from the illegal use of child labor to the payment of wages which amounted to a small fraction of the minimum wage.

Beginning in the late 19th century when the vast majority of ready-made clothing was still being made by people working at home, the progressives and unionists fought for a regulated work space outside the home. The first collective agreement in the New York garment industry was signed in 1910 between the union and the cloak manufacturers. It stated, "No work shall be given to or taken to employees to be performed at their homes." Beginning around the turn of the century a network of local laws and regulations which limited homework were put into effect. Targeted were what people in the garment industry refer to as "the needle trades."

THE SWEATING SYSTEM

Today it is hard to realize the degree to which "industrial homework" was passionately despised by those in the trade unions. One thing which is often forgotten today is that homework was part of the "sweating system" which was the focus of so many labor struggles. One expert described the system this way to a Congressional hearing in the late 1930s:

> It should be noticed that there are two distinct kinds of "sweating," that of the sweat shop proper, where the sweater lives in a room and has a number of men and women working under his direct oversight and that of the home worker, where the head of the family takes work from a sweater, which he carries home to be completed by himself and family.

To those in the International Ladies' Garment Workers' Union and other unions, the tenement workshop—the classic sweatshop of the American history textbook—was an expanded home workshop. What rallied the hatred of homework were cases like this one from a 1936 bulletin of the Pennsylvania Department of Labor and Industry:

> Mrs. K has worked ten years for one firm, earning 2 2/3 cents per hour, knitting baby sacques at $1 per dozen. The retail price of the sacque is 59 cents but the employer answered the protest against the low wage by saying that he "could not make much on the deal."

To say that *homework* represents a red flag to the elders of American trade unionism is to engage in considerable understatement. There are many who claim that union opposition to homework in the 1980s is based on, as the *Wall Street Journal* put it, the desire "to protect unions, not workers." It is not that simple or self-serving. It is a deeply rooted, historical belief based on long-established doctrine. As we shall see, the opposition today is intense, sincere and anachronistic.

STAYING AT HOME

As is so often true with a system neatly in place, this one began to unravel. For a small but significant minority the urge to go to work was replaced by the urge to stay at home and work. The unraveling was not sudden, but rather gradual and steady.

For one thing there was the energy crisis which, if nothing else, got people thinking about the waste of perpetual commuting. Not only was it a source of stress, traffic congestion and air pollution but it was drinking up vast amounts of gasoline. The gas lines of the late 1970s were brought about by a national petroleum shortfall of 3% to 5%. If, as economists and editorialists pointed out at the time, some of us could work at home a day or two a week, the solution would be at hand.

As the price of gasoline rose to more than a dollar a gallon, people who did work at home wrote about how well they survived the gas crisis and the return to normal commuting. More advantages were cited as magazine and newspaper articles told us such things as:

"The savings in transportation costs alone would be enough to finance a vacation. Long lunches and their attendant high checks would be a thing of the past, increasing the worker's productivity and keep-home pay." (George Clifford in the *Washington Post*, February 15, 1977.)

"The rent is right; you can take tax deductions for parts of the mortgage, electric, gas and telephone bills. You get another tax break if you make structural improvements on your house." (Penelope Lemov, *The Washingtonian*, March 1977.)

Even the Small Business Administration got into the act with a brochure pointing out, among other things, "there are many advantages in running a home business...working leisurely in the convenience and comfort of home; missing the hassle of the rush hour commute; reducing bills for transportation and clothing maintenance; and watching the children without the expense of outside day care."

Just as the "rec room" had been the newest necessity of the 1940s and 1950s, the home office came into its own in the 1970s and 1980s. Suddenly, slick magazines were running full-color spreads on the home office complete with photos of VIP home offices and sections on chic home office equipment—an early example was the *New York* magazine 1974 issue on the home office which not only showed us Walter Cronkite's and James Beard's home offices but also featured such basic office equipment as $3,500 Wooton desks and $200 antique inkwells ("can be purely decorative or serve as paperweights"). All of this has been helped by the tax laws which have long allowed deductions for home offices. Starting in 1982 Congress significantly liberalized these deductions for renters and owners alike (although the IRS would still frown on trying to write off your antique inkwells).

Another factor was the great number of women who decided to go back to work but to do so in their own homes. A number of factors contributed to this. In their book *The New Entrepreneurs*, Terri P. Tepper and Nona Dawe Tepper studied 98 women who had opened home businesses. "As the research progressed," they wrote, "the significance of working from home became clear. Women started home businesses because they wanted to stay at home with their children, or because they were divorced, spouses got sick or died, or jobs were unavailable elsewhere—or because a woman determined she was capable of doing better on her own."

A national factor at play has been the fact that day-care and after-school programs have had trouble getting off the ground. After the key Nixon veto which effectively killed the idea of a national day-care system, day-care centers have been in great demand but short supply. Many have made do and given their older children new responsibilities as "latchkey kids" who take care of themselves at home after school. There are now some 6 million of these children in the United States, according to Rep. Patricia Schroeder (D, Colo.), cochairwoman of the Congressional Caucus for Women's Issues, who is behind a new effort to get Federal money to set up child-care centers in the public schools.

If the United States had a vast child-care network as is found in some European countries, the situation might have been different, but to many women working at home seemed like the preferred alternative to baby sitters and latchkey kids. Although many children had no problem with their latchkey status, others, especially urban children, had. Those pushing for Federal child-care money cited not only emotional problems but physical ones. Noting that 6,000 children in the United States between the ages of five and 14 die each year in household accidents including a thousand who die in fires, Sen. Claiborne Pell (D, R.I.) said, "In almost all of these situations, no adult is present."

Some simply performed office or industrial functions at home while other women created businesses which were often extensions of a skill they already possessed, such as a hobby which was turned into a commercial craft. Still others began with an entirely new idea.

Phenomenal stories of kitchen table alchemy started to circulate. The *Christian Science Monitor* told of a woman who earned $120,000 making light figures for dollhouses at her dining room table (adding that her next-door neighbor didn't even know she was working). A *Newsweek* piece on "worksteading" told of a toy business started by a woman in her garage which was now racking up sales of $25 million a year.

It seems that these were not just isolated cases. The Census Bureau, which has tracked women-owned businesses, found that more than half of these, more than 300,000 businesses, were home-based. Of the home-based businesses 357 took in more than a million dollars a year.

COTTAGE CHIC

Concurrently came what *Newsweek* termed "the current chic of handmade goods" which gave new life to quilters, potters, calligraphers, doll makers, pastry makers and dozens of other cottage crafts people who seemed like anachronisms a decade ago. Then came what the guidance counselors termed "alternative professions"—oddball vocations that didn't show up in the Labor Department pamphlets—including such things as gorilla-grams, desk organizers and fantasy brokers. Somebody even figured out that there was money to be made in serving other people breakfast in bed. The anachronistic trade of chimney sweeping made a comeback and, because someone came up with the idea of traveling Renaissance Fairs, there were actually a few people earning a living making armor. Experts were quoted in the papers saying that these "alternative professions" were just a fad and would soon go the way of the hula-hoop. They didn't go away and, if anything, now seem more common than ever before.

Some of these new occupations were not as whimsical as the alternative professions. One of these was that of information broker: individual researchers using large libraries and data bases to provide custom services to business clients. These freelance research librarians have created their own small industry which, according to several estimates, will post annual sales of $100 million a year by the end of the 1980s.

Finally, there emerged a certain idealism to the whole thing expressed in many ways but perhaps best summed up in the word "workstead," which was first used in a book of the same title by Jeremy Joan Hughes. In the introduction to her book, Hughes said that the word embodied the concepts of "independence, self-reliance and pioneering." She added that it meant working and living in the same place but and beyond that "for it emphasizes a scale of activity that gives equal importance to a person's occupation and the essential people and comforts in his or her life." Clearly, this transcended smaller concerns like home office tax deductions and commuting and came closer to a total vision of self, family and society. Hughes wrote, "That worksteads are feasible and timely seems clear; that they are also enormously beneficial to their participants is the payoff. There is a personal dimension to worksteading that surpasses convenience or necessity. When a person lives where he works, he is more able than the 9-to-5 worker to participate fully in family activities, crises and growth."

Yet with all of this, it was hard to come up with an exact idea of how large the homeworking population had become. It is one of the few variables not tracked by the Bureau of Labor Statistics. The only official estimate is that of the Census Department, which showed the number at over 2 million for 1980. Some say that that is an imperfect and outdated estimate and the true amount is much, much higher. Coralee Smith Kern, who heads the National Association for the Cottage Industry, says that the number is actually closer to *10 million*, approaching the 11 million figure cited in an aforementioned 1984 AT&T study.

One reason for the vast disparity in the numbers may be the fact that a lot of people who do work at home may not wish to be counted.

ILLEGALITIES

Fact is that a lot of Americans who work at home do so illegally. Some have, until late 1984, violated Federal rules, others violate state laws and others run afowl of local ordinances. In a heavily regulated place like New York or Massachusetts there are doubtlessly people violating the law at more than one level and a lot of people who are breaking the law probably don't even know it.

The laws are more than minor details, but rather the very issues which in and of themselves will determine the once and future shape of self-employment as an option. Besides the homework laws and regulations there are other considerations ranging from apartment buildings and condominiums which prohibit working on the premises to the vast network of license and permit requirements in force.

Item. A Chicago couple, Patrick and Leah O'Connor, were recently charged with zoning violations for running a word-processing operation out of their apartment. They had violated an ordinance which said that a professional could work at home but "not for the general practice of his profession and not for the installation or use of any mechanical or electrical equipment customarily incident to the practice of such a profession." Columnist Mike Royko, who has championed the O'Connors' cause, has pointed out that if the ordinance were strictly enforced—which the city says it will do in the O'Connors' case—even the use of an electric calculator would be illegal.

The Chicago zoning rules are notoriously bad. While writing his booklet on *Planning for Home Occupations* for the American Society of Planning Officials, William Toner decided to see what the average citizen had to go through when trying to establish the legality of a home profession. He called Chicago's City Hall to say that he was building doll houses in his home and selling them by mail. After a predictable bureaucratic runaround he finally located a man in the zoning department who told him, "You are in violation of the law. You can't do this, and, if someone complains, you'll be in trouble. If you came in to get a permit, they wouldn't give you one." Toner commented, "This was bad news—not so much for me, since I really wasn't in the doll-house business—but for the dozen or so people on my block who really are engaged in occupations in clear violation of the zoning ordinance. Lawbreakers all."

Toner concluded that there are four common problems with local home occupation ordinances: (1) They bear only the slightest relationship to the public interest. ("Many ordinances, including Chicago's, would technically prohibit a person like Saul Bellow from writing full-time in his home.") (2) Most people don't know exactly how to define a home occupation, much less that ordinances exist and that permits may be required. (3) Most people have no idea whom to contact to find out if they are legal and, if they do, won't call because they fear finding out that they are illegal. (4) The language of these ordinances tends to be "clumsy, confused, muddled and vague."

It should be pointed out that these are not always musty regulations from an earlier time, but rules which still get enacted. *USA Today* reported on July 5, 1984 that Lisle, Illinois was then considering an ordinance barring writers from working at home.

Item. Dr. Constance Goldberg, a 37-year-old pediatrician, had fallen into the habit of treating children at her home office in Fairfax, Virginia. According to the *Washington Post* she had saved lives in the neighborhood (including one infant with a heart defect whose life she saved twice). But she was accused of taking people on an emergency basis outside the hours permitted by the zoning board and she was closed down. She confessed to the zoning board that about once every two weeks she had in fact treated an emergency during the banned hours.

Item. Superimposed on zoning issues is a vast national patchwork of professional licensing and permit requirements. More than 150 occupations are licensed. Some are logical and traditional, such as electricians and nurses, but others are less so, beekeepers, tree surgeons, interior decorators, jewelers and people who sell lightning rods. A five-year study of the subject by the Educational Testing Service commissioned by the Department of Labor and published in 1972 concluded it was a field "embedded in a morass of federal, state and local legislation suffused with tradition and jealously guarded rights."

Item. Eighteen states—California, Connecticut, Hawaii, Illinois, Indiana, Maryland, Massachusetts, Michigan, Missouri, New Jersey, New York, Ohio, Pennsylvania, Rhode Island, Tennessee, Texas, West Virginia, Wisconsin—as well as the District of Columbia and Puerto Rico have homework laws in effect. There are some logical prohibitions involved (fireworks, bandages and other sanitary goods) and some which are much less so (Indiana prohibits homework on a long list of things including vests, trousers and overalls, and purses.) Others require licenses, permits or certificates and several have broad, far reaching homework rules. The most restrictive is New York, where all homework is prohibited in all industries, except where the industrial commissioner, after proper study, determines that such work may be permitted without unduly jeopardizing factory workers. If homework is permitted, the homeworker is then required to be licensed. These rules are enforced. The *Wall Street Journal* reported in 1983, "...New York last year forced out of work about two dozen people in a rural part of the state who were putting together cable-television boxes at home in their spare time."

To be sure not all those who are affected by the work-at-home controversy are self-employed; some are technically employed by others. But in this matter self-employment and the freedom to work at home are intertwined.

The issue has been brought into sharpest focus on the national level.

KNITPICKING?

"The Homeworker Song"
(To the tune of "Look for the Union Label")

Look for the union label
'Cause it's illegal for others to knit.
Those evil housewives, make better skicaps;
We break their kneecaps, and send them to jail.
To feed their kids they work hard,
But we're complaining,
It's anti-social, unless you pay dues!
So always look for the union label;
So we can keep this cancer away from you.

Look for the homemade label
We've higher standards than huge factories.
And that's the reason, the unions hate us,
And they berate us and our families.
To feed the kids we work hard,
But who's complaining?
I'll tell you who, the I.L.G.W.U.
So when you're buying, remember fairness
So the American dream can come true.

(Contents of a mimeographed sheet distributed by women protesting ban on homework at hearings on a bill to eliminate the ban, February 9, 1984.)

In 1937 President Franklin D. Roosevelt began fighting for his Fair Labor Standards bill which would effectively make the sweatshop illegal and put an end to most forms of child labor. It would accomplish much toward ending sweatshops by setting a national minimum wage and requiring overtime payments to be made after a worker had worked a certain number of hours. The bill was a major piece of progressive New Deal legislation which Roosevelt pushed every way he could in the face of bitter opposition from those who felt that such regulation was a matter for the individual states. "A self-supporting and self-respecting democracy," Roosevelt told the nation in a May 1937 radio broadcast, "can plead no justification for the existence of child labor, no economic reason for chiseling workers' wages or stretching workers' hours."

Initially Congress refused to act, but the Fair Labor Standards Act was finally passed in June 1938. One important provision of the act was to give the administrator of the Labor Department's Wage and Hour Division the right to set rules banning types of work which violated the intent of the law. In 1942 and 1943 the Department of Labor stated that it was unable to enforce child labor, minimum wage, overtime and safety laws in certain areas and banned homework in seven sewing-related industries—knitted outerwear, jewelry, gloves and mittens, buttons and buckles, handkerchiefs, women's apparel and embroidery.

These were seen as the areas in which exploitation was the worst, especially among immigrant women in big cities as well as the rural poor. The specific nature of the bans was set to get at the most outrageous cases. It was, for example, legal to make men's clothing at home as long as it wasn't knitted. It was also all right for people to engage in homework in the seven banned areas if they were handicapped or were caring for an invalid; but to do this legally, a person needed a permit from the Labor Department.

In 1945 the Supreme Court upheld the right of the Labor Department to effect such bans, and over the years various decisions by the department and the courts have broadened the exact definition of who cannot work at home.

Meanwhile, a number of states established their own "needle trades" prohibitions going beyond Federal law. California and Ohio prohibited homework on any kind of clothing, New Jersey made it illegal to work on infant's and children's clothing and Massachusetts banned all home apparel work except hosiery and women's millinery.

For many years these prohibitions were seen as givens, and they attracted little attention. From time to time, new evidence surfaced showing that home workers tended to be abused by unscrupulous employers. In the late 1950s, for instance, the Labor Department did a survey of legally employed home workers (that is, those not in the banned areas) and found that 3,711 of the 22,580 surveyed were paid under the minimum wage, 800 were not paid enough for overtime and 94 children were found working.

But then in 1980 the Labor Department decided to enforce the ban on home-knitted outerwear against a group of Vermont women who had, for a number of years, been making ski caps in their homes. It did this by suing two small manufacturers who were buying the caps from the women. Ironically, the government stumbled into the case. A women working in the factory, not at home, complained to the Labor Department that she was not getting the minimum wage. A Federal investigator audited the company's payroll records and found that the woman had been properly paid but noted, while going through the books, that the company was paying home knitters. The Labor Department filed suit.

The homework suit created an immediate furor which has not yet died down but which will likely be with us for the rest of the decade. The case of the Vermont women became both a legal tussle and a symbolic one which has brought into question the whole issue of the legality of working at home.

It also brought up the issue of who is and is not a self-employed independent contractor. The Vermont women have steadfastly insisted that they were free and independent. Nancy Smith, in a statement prepared for hearings on the subject, stated, "I am not compelled to knit just for Stowe Woolens. As an independent contractor I can knit for other buyers. I bought my knitting machine and I am responsible for keeping the machine in working order." Another knitter, Christine Brown, testified, "I am able to negotiate the price of every hat and sweater, the knitters all get together, and without a union and the cost of that." Those who fought to maintain the ban argued that the knitters were nothing less than industrial pieceworkers laboring outside the law.

What has gradually become clear here was that the stakes transcended the knitters or the seven banned areas of industrial homework, that they had to do with the oft-heard prediction that more and more of us are going to be working at home with each passing year.

LOOMING LARGER

The raising of the Vermont case, among other things, brought about calls for new and vigorous attempts to curtail other forms of homework. The AFL-CIO, for instance, has proposed that the ban be extended into new areas including electronics and computer work and one union has already banned its more than 700,000 members from virtually any form of telecommuting.

The Vermont case was important in that the 50 women involved were unanimous in their anger that they had been "protected" out of long-established jobs by meddlesome regulators who didn't understand the situation. Almost every major newspaper had an article on the case containing quotes from the women pointing out the absurdity of it all. They claimed, as if with one voice, that they were making more than the minimum wage, could work at their own pace, could keep an eye on their children and did not feel at all exploited by the two firms which paid them for their hats. Some pointed out, as did Audrey Pudvah to a reporter from the *New York Times*, that if she had to travel to a job, buy work clothes, pay a baby sitter and get a second car she probably would not work at all. Others could not commute to a job. The *Wall Street Journal* told of Cecile Duffany, an invalid with acute arthritis in her hips, who made 36 hats a week to make $48.60 to supplement the money her husband got from his pension and Social Security. Despite the low pay, she said, "If I couldn't make hats, it would be horrible." Another woman was knitting so the family could afford expensive allergy medicine for her son.

If anything, one could not imagine the Labor Department picking a case in which the workers were less exploited and less willing to be portrayed as victims. Nor did they look like victims when they were shown on network television news sitting in their clean, well-lit homes in the picture postcard setting of rural Vermont. "We take pride in our work and we want to be able to continue to support our families," said one of them on the "CBS Evening News," adding the question, "Would you rather we went on welfare?"

This lack of identifiable victims was most forcibly driven home when the Labor Department convened for two days of hearings on the matter in Burlington, Vermont and affected women came out in 30-degree-below-zero weather to tell their protectors to get off their backs. One woman pointed out that her family's home knitting business began when the U.S. government had given her mother, now 85, a knitting machine and instructions for making socks for GIs. She brought the instructions with her and told the investigators, "The laws need changing, not our lives." Others pointed out that some of the knitters had been guided to the business by another government agency, the state's Department of Rehabilitative Services, while a witness representing the United Church of Christ said that his church's development group had determined that home knitting was often an important factor in avoiding poverty.

One of the manufacturers, C. B. Vaughan Jr., took the opportunity to say that if the ban was upheld he would either stop making the hats or set up a plant in Asia. The second manufacturer, David Putnam of Stowe Woolens, said that the ban could put his small company out of business. After initial-year sales of $160,000, the company's sales dropped to $110,000 when the Labor Department cracked down on the knitters. "If the homework regulations are not changed, we might not have a third year," Putnam testified. He also said, "Inflation has made the single-wage-earner family obsolete. Yet a person with domestic responsibilities—kids, cows, elderly relatives or whatever—cannot leave home and earn money."

While the Vermont witnesses, including a representative of the governor, argued in favor of dropping the ban, officials from the labor departments of Connecticut, New York and Massachusetts took the opportunity to argue against lifting the bans. The New England regional director of the AFL-CIO not only supported the existing ban but brought up the issue of extending it to other industries, such as electronics. He pointed out that homework bans would not eliminate jobs "but, on the contrary, will result in transfer of the scene of their work from the home to the factory, and will do this without undue hardship."

There was extensive coverage of the hearings, with the press clearly siding with the knitters against the government and the unions. "Has Big Government run amok?" asked *Newsweek*, answering, "The case might lead to a consideration of just who needs Big Brother's help."

After the Burlington hearings, additional hearings were held in Washington, D.C. A group of knitters raised money, some from the sale ofbumper stickers reading "Let Knitters Do It At Home," so that they could be heard again. In addition the Senate Education and Labor Subcommittee on Labor Standards held hearings on the issue in Washington, Los Angeles and New York. With these hearings more individuals and institutions were brought into the discussion. The National Consumers League argued for the extension of the ban into all areas and dismissed the knitters' case as one involving untruthful public relations. This group pulled out every imaginable stop in its argument including the warning that "even the public may be harmed if a contagious disease is transmitted to them via the home-manufactured product."

Meanwhile, a group of the women with the help of the conservative Center for National Legal Policy was suing the Labor Department for the right to begin knitting again. One of their central arguments was that by making home knitting illegal the government was denying them the protection of minimum wage and hour laws which are at the core of the FLSA. They reasoned that those working in a prohibited area would not report a wage or hour violation because it would result in the immediate elimination of their job. If the job was legal, they would have no reason not to complain.

On May 1, 1981, after hearings in Burlington and Washington, D.C., Labor Secretary Raymond Donovan said he was thinking of rescinding the ban in the Vermont case based on the finding that those workers had not been exploited. He also suggested that all the homework bans were unnecessary and announced that he was formally proposing to end them all. The proposal was published in the *Federal Register* on May 5 inviting public comment.

The reaction was so strong that the deadline for comment was extended. When the final deadline came, the result was unprecedented: close to 10,000 written comments had flooded the Department of Labor's Wage and Hour Division. There were 3,245 letters written in support of dropping the bans on homework and 6,024 letters in favor of keeping them. Those in favor of the bans included 133 unions, 200 employers, 178 members of Congress and more than 5,000 individuals, almost all of whom identified themselves as union members. Those who wrote to say they wanted the bans dropped were almost all individuals from the New England states. There were also a half dozen letters from New England congressmen and support from the Small Business Administration, which held that the bans "create a substantial economic and administrative burden on small business and do not adequately reflect the current status of industrial homework."

BANNED AGAIN

Meanwhile, as this went on, the Vermont issue was far from settled. On October 8, 1981 the Labor Department announced what was an obvious attempt at a compromise. The bans would remain in six areas but would be lifted in the seventh, knitted outerwear. The women in Vermont hailed it as a victory and went back to their ski caps and sweaters.

Then a group of institutions led by the International Ladies' Garment Workers' Union and including knitted outerwear manufacturers sued to have the knitting ban reinstated. Donovan's decision was upheld by the Washington, D.C. District Court, but the union appealed and in November 1983 the ban was reinstated by the U.S. Court of Appeals, which ruled that Donovan's ruling was "arbitrary and capricious." The Vermont women and those who employed them were now back at square one. The court did not find any abuse of the knitters and was clearly quibbling with Donovan's procedural approach. It also held that the Labor Department must get Congressional approval to change the rules. In March 1984, Donovan said that the women could go on knitting, in defiance of the first court order. He let it be known that he would initiate a new attempt to have the rules changed and was immediately sued by the ILGWU.

In May of 1984 the Supreme Court upheld the lower court ruling and the ban remained. The Labor Department reiterated its desire to have the bans off the books and the Republican party seconded this when they added it to their platform for 1984.

The Vermont women were allowed to work illegally while the legal appeals continued setting up the question of what would happen if the ban was ultimately upheld. As the *Wall Street Journal* put it in a December 6, 1983 editorial, "Would the court have us believe that these Vermont housewives present a clear and present danger to the nation? Should they be hauled out of their homes and tried if they insist on their nefarious knitting after their appeals have been exhausted?" The fact is that the bans may be all but impossible to police, or as a Senate aide told the *Castine* (Me.) *Patriot*, it is "as close to being an unenforceable law as you can have."

At this point, a group of legislators led by conservative Sen. Orrin Hatch (R, Utah) introduced a bill called the Freedom of the

Workplace Act (S. 2145) which would virtually eliminate all of the Federal bans on homework. Similar legislation has been introduced in the House by Rep. Ron Paul (R, Texas.)

Predictably, there is a high level of emotion going into some of the arguments. In a 1981 ad in the *New York Times*, United Federation of Teachers President Albert Shanker claimed, "Industrial homework will lure tens of thousands of children from school which offers them a future, a way out of ignorance and poverty, to the kind of work in which they and their families will continue to suffer."

Sen. Donald Riegle (D, Mich.) went as far as to suggest that the issue was created and manipulated by Ronald Reagan to start a war between selfish middle-class women working at home and the exploited urban poor. Riegle's conspiracy theory falls apart when it is recalled that the issue was created by the Labor Department's prosecution of the Vermont cases under President Carter and the first hearings were held while Carter was still in office.

On the other side, there were a few crafts people—of the kind that show up at fairs to sell their stained glass, pottery and hand-tooled leather—who depicted the Labor Department bans as immediate threats and passed the word that organized labor would soon force them to abandon their kilns and home workbenches for a place on the assembly line.

HOMEWORK THEATRICAL

On February 9, 1984 Senate hearings were held on the Hatch bill. The fact that an issue of personal freedom was at stake guaranteed a spirited showing replete with a few sideshows. Women picketed outside the Dirksen Office Building with signs like "I CAN'T TAKE MY BABY TO THE ASSEMBLY LINE" and during the hearing itself there was more than just a touch of what politicians call *posturing*—such as a senator holding up red, white and blue ski caps and asking rhetorically how the production of such a handsome product could be deemed an illegal act in the United States of America. A union official invoked the image of industrial equipment in the home where children are subjected to "swift moving parts and electrical dangers." This was greeted with great laughter from the homeworkers in the audience including one breastfeeding one of her children in such a position as to make the act as much one of symbolism as nutrition.

Some of the people who had shown up were from Deva Natural Clothes, a small home-based sewing group from rural Maryland, which sees itself as the antithesis of the sweatshop. Deva (Sanskrit for "angel") was created by three Southern Californians who decided to enter what is increasingly being termed the world of benevolent capitalism. Their business was seen as a vehicle for self-growth, community self-sufficiency and individual freedom. Clearly, these were people whose notion was not to exploit homeworkers but rather to revert to the old system of artisans working at home.

They located in rural Burkittsville and lined up local seamstresses to make unisex cotton shirts and drawstring pants for yoga and meditation. Déva buys from 18 local women who, it claims, make a minimum of $4.50 an hour and are, in fact, self-employed independent contractors. In 1983 Deva was almost put out of business by a homework ban which had been pushed by the ILGWU in the Maryland legislature and which had already passed in the Senate. At this point Deva hired a lobbyist and helped get the law defeated. It is now working to inform people in other states about similar laws on the books or being proposed in other states. Deva has become a force in trying to get the Federal bans removed. It showed up at the Senate hearings with over 3,000 signatures in support of the Hatch bill.

(An odd moment came in the Senate hearings when an article of unisex Deva clothing was held up to illustrate the point that if you considered it a woman's blouse it was illegal, but if you considered it a man's shirt it was legal. By the same token it was shown that a full-sized home-knitted ski cap was illegal but a smaller version with a loop on it could be legally knitted and sold as a Christmas tree ornament.)

In arguing for an end to homework bans, the clearly countercultural Deva found itself allied with conservative legislators who see the issue as one of classic free enterprise. This odd alliance is par for the course with this issue. Labor-related issues almost always quickly break down into easily identified positions pitting liberals vs. conservatives and organized labor vs. management; but this one features some of the most unlikely couplings to come along in a long time. For instance, the Federation of Apparel Manufacturers, which represents the nation's 5,500 manufacturers of women's and children's apparel, is solidly aligned with the ILGWU in support of the ban. Feminists and conservative senators are another odd coupling created by the homework debate.

Some big manufacturers and trade associations have actually called for new extensions of the bans. Peter J. Jones, senior vice president for the Levi Strauss Company, has expressed his company's belief that the bans should be extended to all branches of the apparel industry and that "permitting industrial homework in any form undermines the Labor Department's ability to effectively enforce provisions of the FLSA as well as other Federal acts designed to protect employee rights." The giant $2.8 billion Levi company argues that the bans help small business, a point which is doubtlessly lost on Stowe Woolens and other small operators. There is an ironic touch at work here in that "the freedom to work at home in your blue jeans" has become a cliche among homeworkers.

PLAYER ROSTER

Besides the participants and forces already mentioned, there are others. Consider these additional actors and influences at work on the issues of Federal, state and local bans.

The National Association for the Cottage Industry

A new, remarkably fast growing group which recruited 42,000 members in its first year, it is headed by Cora Lee Kern, who is fiercely opposed to bans on homework. She clearly believes that homework is a question of personal freedom and lifestyle and has asked her members to send clear and simple messages to the Secretary of Labor, such as "Free the Homemaker." Kern, perhaps with tongue in cheek, has threatened to create her own union to protect the freedom that she believes the other unions are trying to take away. She is now in the process of organizing a watchdog committee in each state to monitor Federal, state and local attempts to stop people from working at home.

The National Alliance of Homebased Businesswomen

This group, which is in contact with some 40,000 women working from their homes, was founded by Marion R. Behr. The group refers to its constituency as the "invisible workforce" and is fighting the bans as unfair—specifically, unfair to women. "Why isn't log cutting, selling for a large company, or TV repair (until recently typical men's work) also restricted work?" asks Behr.

The Center on National Labor Policy

A conservative organization which has taken the lead in opposing work at home bans by representing groups of workers who have been closed down by the Labor Department. The CNLP represented a group of the Vermont knitters and has since sided with a Ripon, Wisconsin retail dress business called the Silent Woman Inc. which buys most of its dresses from local seamstresses. In 1982 the Labor Department charged that the Silent Woman was in violation of the ban on home embroidery and did not comply with minimum wage rules; it was fined $72,000.

The Center, the Silent Woman and the individual seamstresses argue that this is a case of independent contractors working cooperatively. They argue that the women are paid more than the minimum wage and do not violate any regulations. In 1983 the company and ten of its independent seamstresses sued the Labor Department charging that their constitutional rights had been violated. As of this writing the Labor Department was still pressing its case, which was to be heard in district court.

The fact that the government had threatened to close down the company has made the women of the Silent Woman as much symbols of the situation as the Vermont knitters. One interesting variation here is that, unlike the Vermont situation where the women were never factory workers, some of these women were. One of them, Mary Clement, testifying in response to the question of whether the women would not have been better off in a factory, pointed out that some of them "formerly were factory sewers who finally said 'no' to the noise, speed and routine of assembly line work so heralded by the labor unions."

Regional Factions

One clear trend on the issue was first seen in the Northeast where the governors of the more urban, unionized states (New York, New Jersey, Massachusetts) lined up in favor of homework bans while the governors of the more rural states (Maine, New Hampshire, Vermont) have argued for lifting them. This has spread but the pattern remains the same, wiih the predominantly rural areas in opposition to those with a history of sweatshops. For instance, some of the strongest Senate opponents to the bans have been from places like Utah, Wisconsin and Oklahoma. In each case, some local trade or tradition seems threatened. Sen. Don Nichols (R, Okla.) has alluded to the fact that the jewelry-making ban, if continued, could have tremendous impact on the people in his state who make Indian-style jewelry from turquoise.

A number of others lined up in opposition to the bans including the American Farm Bureau Federation, which points out that many of its members engage in various forms of homework as a means of supplementing farm income. The Chamber of Commerce of the United States, whose membership is more than 90% small business (more than 180,000 of its member companies have less than 100 employees), has joined to fight the bans along with the General Federation of Women's Clubs and the U.S. Industrial Council.

Nor is this an abstraction. Most of those opposed to the bans are specifically aware of who will be affected if they are enforced. In testimony before the Senate Committee on Labor and Human Resources Sen. William S. Cohen (R, Maine) said, "Here's an example of how home knitting has helped Maine's economy. In 1974, the town of Bingham's only industry, a plywood factory, closed. In the wake of that closing, a cooperative group of home knitters called KiPi of Maine was formed by women who needed income for their families and who had a skill to offer. KiPi now has 85 home knitters who make anywhere from $50 to $250 per week, depending on how much each individual wishes to work. Although they are paid by the piece, all of the knitters earn minimum wage or better. Many of the knitters live as far as 50 miles from Bingham, so working in their homes is important to them."

What is significant about Cohen's tale of rural Maine is that he was telling the country that these people were violating Federal law and clearly had no intention of stopping. It is also no secret at the Labor Department or in Congress that if one really wanted to push the issue large numbers of violators could be found in many states. A Labor Department source says that the internal estimate of the home knitters working in Vermont alone is at least a 1,000, while published estimates put the total at 2,000.

Several rural politicians have suggested that it might be possible for the Labor Department to simply drop the ban for rural areas while keeping it for urban areas. This, as CNLP attorney Michael Avakian points out, may be unconstitutional: "Regardless of where they live, people have the right to pursue their occupations."

Moreover, it is fairly clear that those who support homework bans are not eager to accept exceptions. When asked by the *New York Times* about an exemption for the Vermont women, ILGWU official Edgar Romney said such an exception would "spread like cancer." He also said, "You would see a migration of workers from New York up Interstate 91 to get in on the homework. And soon people would be cutting each others' throats to get the work." Max Wolf, another ILGWU official, had this to say on the "CBS Evening News" segment about the Vermont situation, "All you go do is open the door and it'll be a fungus, it'll spread like a tide."

There *is* a difference between independent contractors in rural Vermont and the illegal aliens working in squalid *barrio* sweatshops in Miami or Los Angeles, but it is clear that those who support the bans do not make this distinction. It is interesting to note that one of the Vermont women testified that she knitted for 21 different companies, clearly the kind of thing that only an independent contractor could say. It is also interesting that since the original flap one of the Vermont women, Audrey Pudvah, has started her own company called

Audrey's Designs and she, in turn, now contracts with other knitters. This is a clear-cut example of a self-employed person developing her work into a small business and is about as far removed from the sweatshop concept as one can get.

The Press

Clearly, the overwhelming amount of coverage given to the issue by the press has been in favor of lifting the bans or pitched toward the individuals in the Vermont and Wisconsin cases. Outside of the magazines and newsletters published by the unions themselves, it is in fact hard to find anyone with anything good to say about the bans.

"To commemorate this Labor Day," said a *Wall Street Journal* editorial on September 2, 1983, "Mr. Donovan could do no better than to proclaim the right to work at home and lift all remaining federal restrictions." It also said, "The only reason for the continuation of the ban is to protect the unions, not workers." From the outset the *Wall Street Journal* has been in favor of dropping homework bans and has kept close tabs on the Vermont case. It would not be an exaggeration to say that the *Wall Street Journal* has made a small crusade out of this issue.

The fact that the pawns in this battle are almost all women has not been missed by commentators from all over the political spectrum. In most cases it has been seen as an issue which is unfair to women. Commenting on National Public Radio, Connie Marsher viewed it as a feminist issue with the government treating "home-based businesswomen" as "defenseless creatures who need someone else to make their decisions for them." She also said in her June 1983 commentary, "The femininization of poverty is not going to be arrested while the Federal government makes it hard for women to earn money. These antiquated regulations should be eliminated." During the same month, the archly conservative Phyllis Schlafly argued that "the 'women need protection' argument is an obsolete stereotype; women should be presumed as capable as men of making their own contracts for services."

The *Washington Post* has called for the legalization of all homework while ensuring that homeworkers receive decent pay and benefits while the *Arkansas Democrat* has said that homework bans "are not only a gross injustice but as wrongheaded a destroyer of work and self-support as ever came out of the federal bureaucracy." The *Christian Science Monitor* termed the seven existing bans "whimsically Neanderthal" and even *People* magazine has gotten into the act with an article sympathetic to the Vermont knitters which appeared almost four years after the illegal knitting was discovered by the Labor

Department.

Then almost as suddenly as it had hit, the specific issue of home knitting was gone. In November 1984 the Labor Department again attempted to lift the ban by ruling that in 30 days it would be legal to knit at home again. This time there was no fight and the ban died quietly on December 6, 1984. Those who supported the ban made no public comment but it had become increasingly clear that public opinion was on the side of knitters, who were looking more heroic by the day.

The other Federal homework bans remained but barring any subsequent legal challenge, these were expected to die at a later date.

With the knitting issue resolved, it seemed as if the issue of Federal controls over homework was dead. Not so.

TELECOMMUTING BAN?

It is becoming increasingly clear that the knitting issue was a warm-up bout for a title event. Attorney Avakian of the CNLP puts it this way: "The battle is over knitting, but the war is going to be over telecommuting."

Until recently the question tended to be more abstract than real, with lots of people speculating on the potential for telecommuting and electronic cottages. Then several companies started offering home computer work and things got down to basics very quickly. For openers, the AFL-CIO at its national convention called for an immediate national ban on computer homework, except in cases involving handicapped workers. Nor is there any question that the ILGWU in fighting to protect the home-knitting ban is aware of its electronic implications. "We cannot afford to wait for a new history of exploitation, wage and hour violations, child labor abuse, and loss of office and factory jobs to homework in that field," said Sol G. Chaikin, ILGWU president, in reference to computer homework, before a Senate committee.

Meanwhile, several other voices have chimed in with the unionists to question the future of telecommuting. Sandra Albrecht, a University of Kansas sociologist, has questioned to what degree the "electronic cottage" will house a new underclass of underpaid women working at word processors without the benefit of benefits.

All of this became even less abstract in 1983 when the Service Employees International Union (SEIU) representing 780,000 workers effectively banned any form of "telecommuting" among its members. An official of the union told *Computerworld* magazine that the executive board of the union had initiated the ban "because we feel other kinds of homework used to take advantage of workers and that it would be better for people to stay in the permanent and regular work force." When asked about the child-care benefits of telecommuting, the same official held that "...the way to deal with child care and working mothers is to pay them enough so they can afford it on their own, and for employers and government funding in some way to help support child care."

Ironically the general union attitude and the specific SEIU ban have gotten very little attention in all the discussion of telecommuting, especially in the articles which talk of millions of Americans working from home via computer in the near future.

A few have rather blithely predicted that all of the bans, regulations and zoning restrictions will be swept away in the near term. It was concluded at a conference on work held by the World Futures Society in the summer of 1983 that all of these prohibitions would be swept away in the next few years. However, there are those whose feelings are very strong on this matter and they are simply not prepared to give people the right to do industrial homework. There is evidence to suggest that as Federal bans are eliminated they may reemerge in a series of new state laws or an expansion of old homework bans. In 1983, for instance, two states, Illinois and Maryland, considered broad homeworking bans. In both instances, they were defeated but this does not mean they will not be back. The other factor is that 18 states now have bans on the books and as Lee Bellinger, a spokesman for the Center on National Labor Policy, put it, "It is often a lot easier to extend a law than create a new one." Bellinger and others at the Center see the issue of homework as one which will be around for a long time, especially if the urge to telecommute is as strong as the futurists predict. If there are bans and controls exacted on telecommuting, they will have a vast impact on both the employed and the independents who choose the option.

As a finale to all of this, consider the following, which indicate the stakes involved in the drive to telecommute.

—At least 450 companies—and some say more—now offer the telecommuting option. Among the companies offering the option are Control Data Corp., Blue Cross & Blue Shield of South Carolina and New York Telephone. Some have come up with interesting variations. Best Western Hotels is using women at a minimum-security prison in Arizona as booking agents and American Express' Project Homebound lets handicapped people work for the company from their homes.

—A New York-based research outfit, Electronic Services Unlimited, is conducting a major research project into the subject. The basic "Benchmark Study" of the subject costs $8,000 and you can sign up for its reports, newsletters and inquiry service for $8,500 a year (or $7,000 if you buy the "Benchmark Study"). Some of the clients which have signed on include General Motors, Xerox, IBM, Equitable Life, Montgomery Ward and AT&T. One finding to emerge from this work is that in the companies studied telecommuting has brought productivity gains of 30% or more.

—Estimates for the future are high. University of Southern California futurist Jack Nilles has been quoted widely for his conclusion that by 1990 a full 10 million Americans will be telecommuting. Nilles, who has been hired by the State of California to study the effect of telecommuting on energy consumption, has estimated that if 12% to 14% of the workforce telecommuted the nation would save 75 million barrels of oil a year—enough to end the need to import oil. An event such as the Arab oil embargo of the 1970s could push estimates even higher.

—There is an increasing amount of thought being given to the idea that teleworking may develop as an option for independent work for America's elderly. Marvin Kornbluh, a futurist working for the Congressional Research Service, has given this a lot of thought and concluded, "Some new careers for older persons could make use of 'telecommuting' or working at home—part-time or full-time...Careers could entail clerical work, writing, consulting on services of some sort, marketing specialized products, and many other opportunities."

Telecommuting is just one of a number of issues which could have a direct and profound effect on self-employment. Now for a look at some of the other issues.

5

THE FUTURE OF SELF-EMPLOYMENT

Will the Urge Become a Megatrend?

There is a story which has been in circulation for decades telling of a hapless forecaster who studied the early growth of the telephone business in America and confidently predicted that there was virtually unlimited potential for telephone operators. The day would come, according to the prediction, when virtually all the available women in the nation between the ages of 18 and 55 would be saying, "Number, please."

Of course, the prediction was wrong because the forecaster did not anticipate a series of technological developments including direct dialing and automatic switching.

During the 1950s the Department of Labor looked at the inroads being made by office automation and confidently predicted that the number of secretaries in America was about to go into decline. The outlook for the future of this occupation was seen as bleak.

It didn't work out that way. The number of secretaries grew and continues to rise dramatically. During the period from 1972 to 1980, 900,000 new jobs came along for secretaries—the largest numerical increase for any profession—and today the Labor Department predicts that between now and 1990 there will be more new jobs for secretaries than for any other occupation. The 1950s prediction of decline, says a Labor Department economist today, was primarily wrong because the impact of new technology had been overanticipated—exactly the opposite of what went wrong with the telephone operator prediction.

These rather famous examples of bad forecasts illuminate the comment once applied to economic forecasting—it is either impossible or easy, but *never* difficult. Sometimes logic works well in making such predictions and they turn out to be fairly accurate. But there are many which are totally off base—predictions suddenly rendered "impossible" by an unanticipated event, court decision, labor agreement, recession or technological advance. Wild cards or X-factors as diverse as the Arab oil embargo, the 16%-plus prime interest rate, Sputnik and the breakup of the phone company have all had a deep effect on employment patterns.

Some forecasts are influenced by developments which do not make headlines. Labor economist Thomas Nardone of the Bureau of Labor Statistics gives two recent examples. The first is that of shoe repairer. As the price of shoes shot up in the last ten years, it would have been logical to assume that the number of repairers would have shot up too; but instead the number decreased. "People have been throwing shoes away rather than having them repaired," says Nardone, adding, "One reason has been style, a lot of the new crepe soles are extremely hard to replace, and another is that there are no training programs for shoe repairers." His second example is the field of credit management. As the use of credit and credit cards expanded, logic again would have led one to conclude that the number of credit managers would have grown at the same rate, but the number has actually remained at the same level for a number of years. "Computers and the fact that retail stores have centralized their credit operations have kept the number of credit managers close to constant."

Given all of this, however, people still must plan their personal futures and want forecasts even if they have warnings attached. Some of the most commonly asked questions have to do with the decade ahead, the period from 1990 to the year 2000. Will the self-employment option open wider or ebb and where will the opportunities lie? Will there be more part-time jobs and will there be occupations for the self-employed which are little known today?

Fortunately, for those thinking about such questions, a number of people are studying them. They include researchers at think tanks and consulting firms which study the future and those working on the job outlook in government. Unfortunately, the experts don't always agree on specifics. For instance, there is broad disagreement on the impact that such things as robots and telecommuting will have on the workforce. However, there is very little disagreement on some of the broader demographic trends which are likely to have a major impact on the job market of the 1990s.

THE CONTINUING BABY BOOM SAGA

There are no less than seven major trends which have become today's givens in looking at the future of work. These are the factors which show up at every symposium and appear in every report on work in the years ahead and represent the futurist's version of conventional wisdom.

1. The Coming Promotion Squeeze

The babies of the 1946-1961 "baby boom" will be between the ages of 29 and 44 years of age in 1990 and the overall number in that age group will be up considerably. Richard Freeman, a Harvard economist, has reported that 25- to 44-year-olds—which he calls the "prime-age work force"—will have jumped an extraordinary 55% to 60.5 million from the 39 million in the same group in 1975. In the chapter he wrote for *Work in America: The Decade Ahead*, Freeman reports that these figures suggest, among other things, "fierce competition for promotions, coupled with substantial career disappointment for many and the possibility that persons in the 25-44 cohort of 1990, some of whom have already entered the job market and are already suffering from being born in a large group, will receive especially low relative income for their entire lives."

Others echo the opinion that the competition for top jobs will be fierce. Roy Amara, president of the Institute for the Future, argues in a paper entitled *The Future of Management* that the number of people trying for each managerial slot in 1990 will double from the present ten competitors to 20. Not only will this be brought about by the maturing baby boomers but other factors including "delayed retirement of present management incumbents, largely in response to persistent inflation at the 7-8 percent levels; and generally slower economic growth at 2-3 percent per year, limiting the development of new management opportunities."

Virtually everyone who has studied the figures concludes that the effect of this squeeze will be dramatic. Landon Y. Jones has written in his book *Great Expectations: America and the Baby Boom Generation* of "crushing disappointments" ahead for those who hold two common baby boom values: jobs in which they can express themselves and jobs which challenge them. Jane Bryant Quinn summed it up in a 1982 *Newsweek* column: "Pity the baby-boom generation, pampered as children, now released into a world too small for them."

Impact on Self-Employment. Positive: an escape from the squeeze, but only if individuals continue to create their own independent jobs.

2. The Fertility Factor

There will be a decline of over a million 18-to 24-year-olds in 1990 compared with 1975, a trend which Freeman termed "the coming shortage of youth," and others have called the "baby bust." In a recent article in *Industry Week*, Peter Drucker predicted that as a result of low birth rates and the "educational explosion" in the industrialized nations, "young unskilled workers available for traditional manual jobs will be increasingly scarce and by the year 2000 virtually nonexistent." Demographers say that the fertility rate, which has plummeted from 3.8 children per married couple in the late 1950s to 1.8 today, will remain low and perhaps decline further. Ironically, there was widespread assumption in the late 1960s that we were headed into a new baby boom. The figures seemed to support this for 1969 and 1970, but nosedived in 1971 and have stayed low ever since.

A 1982 report from the RAND Corp., *Demographic Challenges in America's Future*, states that the most important reason for these lower fertility rates has been the dramatic increase in women's labor force participation. Eventually, says the report, "The declining numbers, first of young adults, then of the entire adult population, will cause tighter labor markets."

Impact on Self-employment. Negative in the long-run as, presumably, employers sweeten things to attract workers.

3. The Female Factor

By all accounts, there will be an ever increasing number of women in the workplace. The Labor Department estimates that women will account for about two-thirds of the growth in the U.S. labor force between 1980 and 1990, something in the neighborhood of an increase of 11 million women. Others feel that the number will exceed the 12 million who entered the workforce in the 1970s, and the 1980s will see 16.5 million women coming to work for the first time. The RAND study not only says that more women will work but that women will work more hours on the average.

Impact on Self-Employment. Extremely positive as women bid to dominate self-employment. If the 1980-82 period is any barometer this will be soon. During that period the number of self-employed women went up 10% while the number of self-employed men went up only 1%.

4. The Immigration Factor

In addition, the proportion of blacks in the workforce will be larger, fewer workers overall will be members of trade unions, and there will have been a major influx of immigrants—both legal and illegal. The *Washington Post* recently reported, "The current rate of legal immigration alone could add 12 million to the population by the end of the century demographers say. The ranks of illegal immigrants and refugees are likely to swell the work force still further, though the overall impact that would have on the job market is unclear." **Impact on Self-Employment.** Positive, as the traditional path to success for immigrants has been through self-employment.

5. The Collegiate Countertrend

It appears that there will be a surplus of college graduates through the 1980s, but this will ease in the 1990s. "A surplus of between 2 and 3 million college students is expected to enter the labor force during the 1980s," concluded Jon Sargent in a recent issue of the Labor Department's *Occupational Outlook Quarterly*. He also pointed out that the underemployed and unemployed college graduates left over from the 1980s will compete with the 80s entrants. Others have pointed to such factors as the aforementioned "baby bust," increasing college costs and cutbacks in financial aid may lead to a countertrend. According to a report from the consulting firm of Theodore Barry and Associates, called "The 1990 Worker," the nation will produce fewer and fewer college graduates. "The law of supply and demand will become increasingly apparent as employers vie for these highly prized graduates."
Impact on Self-Employment. Initially, positive; then negative.

6. The Era of the Elderly

The sheer number of elderly persons in the society will increase dramatically with the aging of the baby boom—the first wave of which will become 65 in the year 2010. This will have an effect on health-care costs: "If the current US population were distributed by age as it is projected to be in 2035," says the RAND demographic study, "the number of days it would spend in the hospital would be at least 25 percent higher than today. At 1979 prices, that implies an additional annual expenditure on hospital care alone of about $20 billion." It is also given that there will be much greater demands on the Social Security System as fewer younger workers are expected to pay more to support the growing older population. Rep. Barber B. Conable Jr. (R, N.Y.) recently warned of a "generational war" between the baby boom and baby bust generations. One bright spot—the growing number of women paying the full amount into the system—has its dark side as those women will eventually retire and demand full, rather than dependent, benefits.

Impact on Self-Employment. Positive in the sense that a lot of these folks may opt for a second, self-employed career instead of retirement. Negative, in the sense that increased Social Security costs have fallen heavily on the self-employed—more on this shortly.

7. New Workplace Technology

The onrush of more and more sophisticated computers, communications networks, industrial robots and other marvels of the electronic age will have an impact on the way we work. The common consensus is that the traditional office—a centralized, tightly managed paper mill—will become a dispersed electronically linked operation. The traditional factory, on the other hand, will become more and more automated and robotized.

Having said that, there is disagreement as to what it will all mean. Will new technology create or kill jobs? Some see it providing a raft of new opportunities while others believe many human jobs will become obsolete. The debate is not unlike the one in the 1950s which had one side predicting the loss of millions of jobs because of automation and the other saying the impact would not be dramatic. As it turned out, there was no sustained adverse effect from the first wave of automation. Yet, even with this in mind, there are those who say that it will be different this time because the second wave will bring with it the automation of decision making, flexibility, product design and other abilities which humans have traditionally done better than machines.

However, one thing that most people who have studied the subject agree on is that robots will take over jobs. Even here the estimates of loss are widely different. Gail M. Martin reported on these estimates in the *Occupational Outlook Quarterly* and found them as far apart as 440,000 lost jobs by 1990 all the way to 4 million by the early days of the next century. The first estimate is from a University of Michigan study for the Robot Institute of America (which goes on to say that all but 22,000 of those displaced workers will be retrained for other jobs) while the second is from a Carnegie-Mellon University study.

So too is there a debate over the quality of work in the offices and factories of the future. Some feel that the demeaning, dull and soulless elements of work will be swept away electronically while others predict just the opposite. At Congressional hearings on "New Technology in the American Workplace," Judith Gregory, research director of 9 to 5 (the National Association of Working Women), looked at the future of the office and declared, "Office workers will find themselves threatened with many of the same processes of job degradation which undermined the skills and dignity of an earlier generation of industrial workers." She also held that the new technology would add to the problems of clerical workers—most of whom are women—which include low pay, dead-end jobs and discriminatory employment. Looking at the same future, other witnesses at the same hearings saw offices and factories offering higher wages and more fulfilling work. **Impact on Self-Employment.** Some aspects of this are hard to call, but it is clear that telecommuting and cheap electronics favor the self-employed cottage business.

GLUT AHEAD

The sum of these parts is that of a marketplace glutted with baby boomers scrapping for the best jobs in an increasingly middle-aged workforce which will include more blacks, women and foreign-born than ever before. These numbers tell us that the traditional hierarchical workplace will provide few easy career shots and it's going to become much tougher to get past the first rung of the ladder than ever before. Boom times, however, seem to be ahead for those who treat stress and give seminars on Machiavellian principles.

Yet, this picture—and its component forces—strongly suggests a short-term future in which the lure of independence becomes much stronger, especially for those in their prime working years who are not fiercely competitive but still strive for success. Futurist Roy Amara, among others, concurs, holding that one of the factors that will shape the near future will be the growth of individual risk taking and entrepreneurship. He feels that more employees will want to leave their jobs to start their own businesses, and the increase in dual-income families will provide support for such risk taking.

Unlike Amara, many of those who study the future of work are not concerned with the future of self-employment—except as it figures into the picture of telecommuting—and most of what is being written about topics like autonomy, independence, flexibility and even entrepreneurship is discussed in terms of the employed. This had not only been true of books and articles on the future of work, but was shown dramatically in April 1983 when the House Committee on Science and Technology held two days of hearings on the subject of "Job Forecasting." The hearings were aimed at finding out where new jobs would come from. For two days futurists and occupational forecasters talked about all sorts of employment, but nothing was said about self-employment. It was as if it were an alien form or work with no importance to the American economy. What they did talk about were new occupations—geriatric nurses, genetic engineering technicians, holographic inspectors, a host of robot-related jobs and many others—but nothing about what form they would take.

However, those few futurists who have looked at self-employment seem to differ only in the degree to which its future will be a rosy one.

In his bestseller *Megatrends* John Naisbitt notes the entrepreneurial boom of the late 1970s and sees a shift taking place from a managerial society to an entrepreneurial one led by baby boom adults. He writes: "Their numbers made them a megageneration, an army that was not easily absorbed in society. And the 1970s, when their ranks hit the job front, were not exactly booming times. Consequently, some baby boomers were forced into self-employment, even entrepreneurship, by a weak job market. Others, who had cherished independence in the 1960s and given it up for high-paying corporate jobs in the 1970s were, all the while, saving, learning, and plotting their escape into entrepreneurship." Naisbitt sees this as a continuing phenomenon which will shape the rest of the century.

Interestingly, Naisbitt's research has led him to the conclusion that there are five places—California, Florida, Colorado, Connecticut and Washington—in which new trends start and gradually effect all 50 states. Using this "bellwether state" method of looking at the future, it is interesting that all five of them have shown a substantial increase in the number of self-employed in the period from 1975 to 1980. In three of them, California, Connecticut and Washington, the growth of self-employment far exceeded that of wage and salary workers during the 1980-82 period. In the most dramatic case, Washington, wage and salary employment fell off 1.8% while non-farm self-employment went up 4.2%.

Alvin Toffler, of course, has been at the forefront in seeing the change. In 1970, when his *Future Shock* was published, the conventional wisdom was to declare the end of entrepreneurial America and the total ascendancy of the bureaucratic system. Toffler, however, saw it differently and predicted the rise of risk taking and a new entrepreneurial spirit (which would start within the corporation). By the time *The Third Wave* was published in 1980, he was talking about "the electronic cottage" and other facets of the new independence. To say that he is optimistic about all of this is to understate the case considerably.

Toffler also looks at the 350,000 home-operated, women-owned businesses in the United States and, in his recent book *Previews and Premises*, says, "That's been a little undiscovered island in the economy, accounting for literally billions of dollars of business. And it's operated without any technological support. Now, suddenly, give it cheap computers, cheap telecommunications, video equipment and the like, and I believe it will explode."

If these well-known futurists are bullish on self-employment, so are others who look at it from a different angle. Bruce Phillips, a Small

Business Administration economist who has studied self-employment data, says, "We've seen that self-employment tends to grow in bad or uncertain economic times, so it would seem that the only thing that I can see that will dampen the trend to self-employment is five or six years of strong economic growth." Phillips also feels that the fact that a large number of people—perhaps 25% of the workforce—are *underemployed* will beckon more people to become self-employed. "A lot of these people are beginning to realize that they are stuck in a job that does not fit their abilities and this situation is not going to change in the immediate future."

Phillips also believes that the aging of the population is another force which will add to the ranks of the self-employed. "These are healthier, better educated people who dream about second careers and will work past age 65 whether or not they have to."

One who agrees with this assessment is Marvin Kornbluh of the Congressional Research Service, who has looked at the impact of electronics on various aspects of the society. "I'm convinced that as more and more people become computer literate, the more people will start their own businesses. A lot of these people will be over 60."

SELF-STARTERS

There are other positive barometers including opinion polls and surveys in which the urge to be self-employed or to go into small business ranks high. Most significantly, some 3,300 high school seniors were recently surveyed by the University of Michigan about how they wanted to work. They preferred *self-employment above all*, followed by employment in a small business. Working for specific large institutions (big business, government, the military, etc.) was much further down the list. If nothing else, this survey may shed light on the reason why the age of the average self-employed person is going down in a society which is aging.

Compare the Michigan finding to what William H. Whyte, Jr. reported in his 1957 classic *The Organization Man*. Speaking of college seniors, he wrote, "The urge to be a technician, a collaborator, shows most markedly in the kind of jobs seniors prefer. They want to work for somebody else. Paradoxically, the old dream of independence through a business of one's own is held almost exclusively by factory workers..."

Today 150 business schools offer courses in entrepreneurship—as opposed to ten in 1967—and that elective has been the most popular at the Harvard Business School in recent years. Another indicator of the growth of self-employment is reporttd by Karl H. Vesper of the

University of Washington in *Entrepreneurship and National Policy*: "A sampling of Babson College alumni 8 to 10 years after graduation found that only 14 percent were content to be working for someone else, the remaining 86 percent having indicated preference for owning their own businesses."

The great popularity of self-employment as shown in these studies is part of a larger picture boding well for the future, which is the new attitude toward self-employment, small business and the entrepreneurial, risk taking spirit—all mixed together in one positive predilection for that which is small, individualistic and unbureaucratic.

John Sloan, president of the National Federation of Independent Businessmen, put it this way: "Small business and entrepreneurship are currently riding a crest of popular support. Small entrepreneurs are the 'good guys' doing 'good things' for an economy and society which have struggled over the last several years. Entrepreneurs are once again believed to be the future; bureaucracies are for the first time believed to be the past." The result has been what Vesper has termed the "radical rise of entrepreneurship" and what the *New York Times* in 1984 called America's latest culture hero, the new breed of entrepreneur.

Many forces have shaped this new attitude but nothing has been quite so important as the series of discoveries which have underscored the importance of smallness in our big economy. Sloan credits a great deal of the popularity of small business to the discovery of MIT Professor David L. Birch that it was small, independent business which had created most of the new jobs in the economy between 1969 and 1976. Birch's findings, published in his 1979 book *The Job Generation Process*, were proven again by several other university studies and stunningly updated by Peter Drucker in early 1984 in the *Harvard Business Review*. He noted that between 1981 and 1983 the *Fortune* 500 companies lost 3 million jobs in the United States while small business added a million.

An issue that may have an impact on this is that of the disbanding of the Small Business Administration proposed by the Reagan Administration in early 1985. As this was written the battle lines on that issue were just being drawn, so it is hard to say what the eventual outcome will be; however, if the SBA is abolished there will be one less source of information and loans for the self-employed and small business. The loss might not be devastating as much as it would be very inconvenient.

If small business is one step removed from self-employment it is not a giant step. After all, people at the Small Business Administration are fond of terming it "the smallest form of small business." But in terms of the future there are distinctly different threats to self-employment and small business. It is, for instance, a given that policies aimed at drying up sources of venture capital—and the capital gains incentives that come with it—could have a devastating effect on the future growth of small business. The equivalent threat to self-employment could be its use as a special source of new fees and taxes. A prime example is at hand.

THE TAXATION OF INDEPENDENCE

If nothing else were to change in the tax structure over the rest of the 1980s, one thing is certain and that is that self-employed Americans will pay significantly more each year in taxes than their employed counterparts. As the law now stands, in 1990 a self-employed person will pay a full 15.30% in self-employment tax while the employed person will pay half that amount in Social Security payments. The new payment schedule, enacted in 1983 as part of a larger "rescue package" created to save the system, replaced an old schedule left over from an earlier rescue attempt made during the Carter Administration.

The exact schedule looks like this:

Year	New Schedule	Previous Schedule
1984	14.00%	9.35%
1985	14.10	9.90
1986-7	14.30	10.00
1988-9	15.02	10.00
1990 and after	15.30	10.75

The Social Security Administration estimates that the revised percentages will give the system an additional $18.5 billion for the OASDI (Old Age Survivors and Disability Insurance) fund and $8.3 billion for the HI (Health Insurance) portion. The self-employed will be given a tax credit through 1989 and, after that, a deduction equal to half the self-employment tax.

The rationale behind this was to make the self-employed pay a full share of the tax—the employee's share and the employer's share. The idea was originally proposed by the National Commission on Social Security Reform and passed by Congress. This replaced a formula by which the self-employed paid approximately 75% of the combined shares. From the time when the self-employed were belatedly let into the system in 1950, it was assumed and borne out statistically that they retired later than hired workers. As the U.S. Advisory Council on Social Security put it when it first set up the formula: "The later retirement age which characterizes the self-employed will lengthen their contribution period, reduce the number of years they receive retirement benefits, and result in a savings to the trust fund."

Critics thought that letting the self-employed into the system would get them to start retiring with everyone else, but it didn't work out that way. As recently as 1976 the Social Security Administration studied this and reported, "...the empirical findings that people with a substantial history of self-employment are, indeed, more likely to forego retirement benefits—at least at ages 65, 66, and 67—than are persons with no self-employment."

So given the fact that the self-employed were paying more than other workers, paying it longer and taking less in benefits, Congress decided they should pay an even higher percentage of their earnings starting in 1984. If there was stated logic that this was fair, it was totally lost on the self-employed who saw it as a system forcing one individual to pay twice as much as another with the identical income. In reality, it works out worse than that because the way it is configured, it means that a barber making $35,000 pays twice as much as a corporation president making 15 times as much.

But what if the tax on independence goes even higher? What if there is need for still another rescue package? A third rescue is not as farfetched as it may sound. Less than a year after the system was rescued in 1983, the non-partisan Committee for Economic Development concluded that the rescue assumed very favorable economic conditions and provided "very little margin of safety" against errors. This is even more chilling when one recalls that Congress deemed the 1977 rescue effort capable of keeping the system rolling right into the 21st century.

If recent history is any guide the self-employed will be called on to pay a disproportionate share of these costs. What's more, as the self-employment tax rises in the next few years, it will become clearer and clearer that Congress has so structured things that the entrepreneur in the lower tax brackets will pay more than those in the top brackets. If Congress continues to look on the pool of self-employed workers as the source of Social Security bailout, the situation could become much worse and one more rescue could have disastrous results.

In addition there is the problem of Medicare, which is facing the same funding problems as Social Security was a few years back. In late 1973, Rep. W. Henson Moore (R, La.) called future Medicare financing "the single most important domestic issue facing Congress this decade." The generally agreed upon moment at which the system will go bankrupt is in 1990. One needs no crystal ball to figure out that at least part of the solution could be to increase the amount of money paid into the system by working Americans. Under the provisions of the 1983 reform the Health Insurance (HI) portion of Social Security has already been doubled. The self-employed already pay 2.60% of income (up to 2.90% in 1986) while the employed pay 1.30%, with an equal amount coming from the employer. Even *with* this boost—assuring $8.3 billion from self-employed taxpayers alone by 1989—the HI fund will fall 19% short of outlays by 1990. By 1995 it is expected to be short $252 billion.

In early 1984 the House Ways and Means Committee sponsored a conference on the future of Medicare at which several alternative financing plans were discussed. One was to again increase the HI payroll tax. Some of the other methods hold promise—additional excise tax on liquor and tobacco, a value-added tax and higher general taxes—and the self-employed can only hope that one of these is used lest they have to double the ante again.

It is also possible that the growing number of self-employed people will fight this, especially as it sinks in that they are paying more than other individuals while taking out less in benefits.

CLOUTLESS IN LOBBYLAND

However, the ability and willingness of the self-employed to have a say in all of this are glaringly lacking if the events of 1983 are used as a barometer. As the self-employment tax went up, only a few self-employed voices were heard and these represented only a miniscule proportion of the self-employed. Representatives of only five groups representing a mere handful of self-employed people even bothered to testify before the various hearings held on the subject and only one of them, the National Association of Realtors, made what could be considered a major presentation on the subject. Several farmers groups added their opposition, as did an Amish leader (the Amish are not only predominantly self-employed but oppose the system to the extent that they pay into it but take no payments from it) and a representative of the Small Business Service Bureau, a group that is about half self-employed and half small business. Francis X. Doyle, of the latter group, said later that he was shocked by the fact that so few self-employed people had anything to say—pro or con—about the new tax.

It is instructional to take a look at the testimony of one group that bothered to mount more than a passing negative glance at the increases because it shows the number of good arguments which could be legitimately made against the new tax. Jack Carlson, vice president and research director for the Realtors, in hearings before the House Ways and Means Committee focused on the fact that the proposed change would severely penalize the self-employed who already have no unemployment insurance and are unable to deduct health insurance premiums (as corporations can). Looking at its effects, he came up with this list of negatives:

> The Commission's proposed tax increase on self-employed workers would:
> Be grossly unfair and discriminatory;
> Greatly increase the tax burden on lower income workers;
> Be unfair to self-employed workers in every state;
> Penalize the smallest of small businesses;
> Increase business concentration;
> Discourage the dream of self-employment for many Americans;
> Discourage inventive and energetic workers;
> Reduce the incentive for self-employed workers to continue with
>   a full and productive life; and
> Be unfair towards women.

In each case he came up with a persuasive argument in support of the point. For instance, in the case of the new tax being unfair to women, he showed that if current trends continued women will dominate self-employment in the year 2010 and be forced to pay $800 million annually over and above that paid by an equivalent number of wage and salary workers.

Although a few others, including the National Taxpayers Union, agreed that the self-employed would be unduly burdened, Congress went along with the commission's recommendations and upped the payments. The head of the National Taxpayers Union, James Dale Davidson, in arguing against the new self-employment tax, speculated, "Perhaps the commission felt the self-employed are rich." He went on to show that in 1980 almost half of the self-employed earned less than $15,000. The same speculation could be made about Congress.

There is also some historic irony in all of this. Congress excluded the self-employed from the Social Security system from its inception in 1935 until 1950 when they were finally voted in. Some were willing to stay outside the system but others such as farmers (led by the National Farmers Union) begged to be admitted. For years they were kept out because of the inability of Congress to come up with a way for them to pay. Now that they are part of the system Congress has found a way for them to pay. Twice.

RETIRING WAYS

Meanwhile there is another question on the horizon which has a direct bearing on this. It is this: to what extent will the retirement at age 65 norm of the last 30 years reverse itself? Simply stated: a higher average retirement age benefits self-employment. This is not only true in terms of self-employment second careers but also in terms of lessened pressure on the Social Security system. Consider the following:

- In 1950 nearly half the men 65 and over were in the labor force, but today only 19% are. This trend may be reversing. In 1978 Congress did away with the long established mandatory retirement age of 65 for most workers and reestablished it at 70. The effect of this has been simply that an employer cannot force someone to retire just because the person is 65. Based on a major study of the effect of this rule, the Urban Institute has concluded that by the year 2000 an additional 217,000 men will be in the labor force because of the ruling. This is a modest rise but is just one of a number of factors which could reverse the trend.
- When the Social Security system was created in 1935, the average life expectancy was 62, but the system was set for a retirement age of 65. Today life expectancy is 74 and rising, yet 40% of the people coming onto the Social Security rolls are 62. Congress is not only aware of this but is clearly moving in the direction of adjustments which could reverse it. In early 1983 Congress took the first step when the House voted to raise the age for full Social Security benefits from 65 to 67 early in the next century and the Senate called for a raise to 66 by the year 2015. The final compromise was to gradually increase the retirement age from 65 to 67 by the year 2027. The age would first be raised to 66 over a six year period ending in 2009.

Both houses agreed to allow people to continue to be able to retire at 62 but sharply reduced the benefits available at that age. Beginning in 1990, those who wait until after they are 65 will get a gradual increase in benefits. This "delayed retirement credit" will be cut off, however, if the person retires after age 70.

- Another factor is the growing body of opinion that suggests that early retirement is not the bed of roses it has been cracked up to be. For instance, these days one is hard pressed to find articles in the popular press extolling the golden years of sleeping as late as you want and unlimited time for crafts and hobbies. What you are more likely to find are articles like "The First Step to the Cemetery," a bitter *Newsweek* "My Turn" essay in which the author likens retirement to suicide, and "Why I'd Rather Work," an article in *Parade* in which the author tells why he went back to work after a disastrous retirement in which strange ailments developed and his dreams became angry dreams. A 1979 Lou Harris poll indicated a reversing opinion of retirement, with a majority of those polled indicating that they plan to work past the normal retirement age.

Taking all of these factors together, there is a growing body of opinion which says that the average retirement age is destined to go up. James Jorgensen, author of *The Greying of America* and *Your Retirement Income*, has looked at all of this and concluded, "The ultimate answer is, of course, a gradual rise in the retirement age—up to at least sixty-eight, possibly higher, by the end of this century."

If this happens it will represent a dramatic shift from the days not that long ago when it appeared that the mean retirement age was destined to drop with every report of longer life expectancy. During the Bicentennial in 1976 there were numerous forecasts of the American future. Astonishingly, there were some futurists willing to predict that the *common retirement age for the white-collar worker in the year 2000 would be 40*. This now far-fetched prediction did not appear in some supermarket check-out line tabloid but in the *New York Times* (February 19, 1976, page 40).

"THE LEISURE PROBLEM"

In a broader sense, we may be witnessing a retreat from the long-held vision that the future was a jurisdiction where one of the major social concerns would be how people would deal with excess leisure time as both the importance of work and the time spent working declined. In their monumental book *The Year 2000* the late Herman Kahn and Anthony J. Wiener talked about work in that year from the perspective of 1967. Many in the year 2000 will chose not to work, others will use it for income and fulfillment, but it will have been de-emphasized to the point that "the man whose missionary zeal for work takes priority over all other values will be looked on as an unfortunate, perhaps even a harmful and destructive neurotic. Even those who find in work a 'vocation' are likely to be thought of as selfish, excessively narrow, or compulsive." Conscience and other "Puritanical" values will have disappeared in this world and guilt would now be attached to such vices as achievement and vocational success. They added, "There would then be considerable cultural support for feelings ranging from indifference to outright contempt for any sort of success or achievement that has economic relevance." By the standards of the entrepreneurial 1980s, this vision of the future is rendered ridiculous—especially for a time only 15 years down the road. Success and achievement are very much with us and the major change is that people have begun to customize their definition of success by demanding it on their own terms.

Nobody is fretting about the problems of excessive leisure anymore, and if there are things of this nature worth fretting about, they tend to be traditional problems like interest rates, inflation and the like. For the self-employed there are these as well as things like homework bans, licensing problems and special taxes.

If all of this points in one direction it is that the cost and local red tape involved in self-employment will go up. One factor that could work to keep these under some control would be the increasing power of the self-employed to lobby and effect legislation. Small business has become a powerful force; yet the self-employed, who by one reckoning are responsible for 19% of the Gross National Product, are woefully lacking in this regard. This inability, over time, could have a devastating effect. If there are even stirrings of a self-employed self-interest, it has been in the area of fighting industrial homework bans, but even here much of the energy going into fighting the bans is coming from experienced right-wing lawyers interested, ultimately, in the ideology of defending individuals against an intrusive bureaucracy and a meddling union clinging to an anachronistic, once-noble principle.

In fact, there are very few cases in recent memory when more than a few self-employed got together to defend their interests. One of the few occurred in 1982 in Connecticut when the state passed an absurdly unfair unincorporated business tax which taxed unincorporated self-employed earning more than $50,000 but left a person with a $250,000 corporate salary free of taxes. The self-employed—including a number of articulate non-corporate writers, among them Arthur Miller, Theodore H. White and William Styron—along with groups with self-employed members such as the Small Business Service Bureau got the law repealed.

With the Connecticut case as a good omen, the future of self-employment seems bright. Though there is something especially fascinating about trying to dope out the future of how we will work, it is also fraught with special danger for the simple reason that people are involved and people love to disobey social forecasts. It is a lot easier to make a purely technological forecast as to how many circuits will fit on the head of a pin in the year 2000.

Recall that ten years ago John Kenneth Galbraith and others were calling small and independent business an anachronism in the face of the new industrial state. Recall too that the corporation was supposed to change to make way for all those young people of the late 1960s and early 1970s who were not that pleased with the status quo. One popular, widely quoted future scenario, presented at the White House Conference on the Industrial World Ahead in 1972, described the life of a white-collar worker named Ron in the year 1990:

> Those who are twenty years old today and who are disenchanted with the corporation will be thirty-eight by 1990. Certainly in the interval, the youth of today—many of whom lack career aspirations—will have found that corporate life is not all that bad. The corporation will change during the next twenty-eight years and through its sound action programs, will prove to youth that it is relevant.
>
> Ron Adams will be spending 10% of his time working in the public sector...His corporation may loan him to social service organizations for six months a year, while paying his salary in full.

Not only is it not working out quite like that, but Ron may have already strayed from the corporate paddock and now be spotting his first gray hairs in the reflection in the window of his natural foods shop or in the screen of his desktop computer which he works on at home. Maybe, Ron concluded that the scenario was right in that "corporate life is not all that bad," but reasoned that neither was it all that good.

THE GOOD "BAD FORECAST"

Recalling also that one of the common forecasts of the 1960s and early 1970s was that self-employment was on its way out as an American option, one must then wonder if, perhaps, the forecast itself helped motivate people to say the hell with it and get in before the option door was shut. It slammed open. May it stay that way.

APPENDIX: WHO ARE WE?

An Almanac of
American Self-Employment

The term "self-employed" is likely to evoke parochial images. People in the investment industry tend to look upon the self-employed as a vast and ever growing source of Keogh money, others think of them as a corps of artistic urban freelancers, while the term is sometimes thought of as a synonym for the smaller side of small business. In rural areas, the term naturally attaches itself to farming, and where there's a scent of salt air, there's a tendency to think of it in terms of commercial fishing or drug smuggling.

Congress, it would seem, sees the self-employed as an easy and unprotesting source for extra Social Security revenue and to the Internal Revenue Service the term is, in part, a cover for the underground economy. In beer commercials they are wildlife photographers and other rugged outdoorsmen who say, "I never was much of a company man." To a personnel officer the term is often taken to mean "between jobs" (as in "I've been self-employed since being let go six weeks ago, but I'm getting tired of it and thought it was time to start looking for a job").

Not having a clear picture of the self-employed workforce is dangerous. Those who see them as rich surgeons and lawyers find it easier to tax them, while those who see them as flighty, marginal operators find it easy not to take them seriously. As it becomes clearer and clearer that the self-employed are more than a sociological curiosity but a significant force in the American economy, it is important for them to be understood as a coherent whole.

For the self-employed themselves, it is important to have an idea of the collective whole as well as having an idea of how one fits into the picture as, say, a woman, an Iowan or a person who is over 60.

In order to get a much truer and more detailed picture of the self-employed American, and put some of the vagueness aside, I decided to see what could be coaxed and cajoled from the mountains of largely unpublished government statistics on employment. I hoped to be able to find out enough to get a good picture of the subject—put some flesh on the term "self-employed American." Here it is in words, numbers and graphs organized in terms of the questions which are most logically asked but seldom answered.

Be forewarned, there will be a lot of statistics laid out before this chapter ends, but they will allow readers a number of chances to see where they fit into the picture. Think of it as an almanac for self-employment.

1. Does anyone know exactly how many people in the United States are self-employed?

Not exactly.

The detailed information which the government has collected on our working lives is detailed to an unbelievable degree. The Census Bureau, for instance, can tell us how many Americans of Asiatic extraction sell used cars in Idaho. It is not surprising then that there is much information collected on self-employment. The problem, however, is that a question as simple as how many self-employed people are there gets you vastly different answers depending on who you ask. Here are four different answers:

- 8,735,000. This is the figure used by the Census Bureau based on the 1980 Census.
- 9,778,000. This is the number of people who paid the self-employment tax in 1980.
- 9,170,000. This is the February 1985 total from the Bureau of Labor Statistics.
- 13,000,420. This is the number of Schedule C sole proprietorship tax filings made to the IRS in 1981.

One can throw out the last figure because it counts a number of people who also have regular jobs but file Schedule C tax forms for side businesses. The Bureau of Labor Statistics figure may be the best because it is recent and only counts a person once in their prime occupation. The problem with that figure is that it does not count the private one-person corporations or partnerships.

Consider the fact that there are a minimum of 2.8 million private corporations (this based on BLS statistics for the year 1982 and certainly higher by now) which are one-person operations and are really a form of self-employment even though the owner is technically an employee of the corporation. It is, to quote a Labor Department analysis, a "technical distinction." Because of incorporation the overall increase in self-employment has been even greater than indicated by the basic statistics.

In addition, consider the fact that there are 1.5 million partnerships comprised of some 8.4 million partners. Some are, of course, large, complex operations but others are nothing more than a pair of self-employed, a mom and pop partnership or a self-employed individual with a partner who is actually an investor. There are also some 600,000 family workers who work unpaid for family businesses. The number of unpaid family workers has been going down for several decades but they still must be counted. It would therefore seem fair to conclude that there are at least 3 million more than the strictly defined statistics show.

(Presumably, the number goes even higher if you add the self-employed who are in the underground economy and pay neither taxes nor Social Security and do not report themselves as self-employed to the Census Bureau or any other government agency. The number is not large as most people polled are not asked about taxes but rather about what they do for a living.)

2. What are the general areas of strongest self-employment?

The traditional assumption is that self-employment has been most heavily supported in the service industry, sales and agriculture. This apparently has been true and remains accurate in the latest statistics.

According to the Bureau of Labor Statistics there were 9,143,000 self-employed in the United States in 1983. They are broken down into the following broad categories in descending order:

Services	3,195,000 self-employed, or 10% of 30,922,000 total employment
Wholesale and retail trade	1,932,000 self-employed, or 9% of 21,144,000 total employment
Agriculture	1,565,000 self-employed, or 46% of 3,383,000 total employment
Construction	1,158,000 self-employed, or 19% of 6,149,000 total employment
Finance, insurance and real estate	533,000 self-employed, or 8% of 6,511,000 total employment
Manufacturing	371,000 self-employed, or 2% of 19,946,000 total employment

| Transportation, Communication, other public utilities | 323,000 self-employed, or 5% of 6,987,000 total employment |
| Mining | 29,000 self-employed, or 3% of 921,000 total employment |

3. To what degree have the number of self-employed in various areas risen or fallen in the last decade?

In 1973 the figures were as follows showing the extent to which the picture was to change within a decade:

Services	2,224,000 (up 971,000 for '83, a 43% increase)
Wholesale and retail trade	1,669,000 (up 263,000 for '83, a 15% increase)
Agriculture	1,780,000 (*down* 215,000 for '83, a 12% drop)
Construction	810,000 (up 348,000 for '83, a 42% increase)
Finance, insurance and real estate	301,000 (up 232,000 for '83, a 77% increase)
Manufacturing	260,000 (up 111,000 for '83, a 42% increase)
Transportation and public utilities	193,000 (up 131,000 for '83, a 67% increase)
Mining	15,000 (up 14,000 for '83, a 93% increase)

It is interesting to note that a common reason cited for the growth in American self-employment has been the opportunities in the service fields, especially computers, education and health care. These figures show that it is a strong, healthy factor, but hardly the exclusive factor that some have made it out to be. The only area in which there has been a fall has been in agriculture, where the erosion has been constant for many years. An SBA study of self-employment from 1960 to 1975 came to this conclusion: "The finance, insurance and real estate industry was the leading gainer, followed by services. Somewhat smaller gains were evident in construction, and transportation, communications and public utilities. Some small losses were noted in retail trade, and manufacturing, while significant declines were evident in wholesale trade."

4. What is it, exactly, that we do for a living?

It is perhaps the most important and fascinating question, and the answer tends to dispel a large number of myths. Based on unpublished Bureau of Labor Statistics data, here is how it all breaks down. These figures are for 1983 and take into account all 9,143,000 in both non-agricultural and agricultural fields. As the total working population for 1983 was 100,832,000 the percentage of self-employed is almost exactly 9%.

Managerial and Professional Specialty Occupations

Some 2,437,000 people, or about one-tenth of the total in these professions. The areas in which there are more than 10,000 self-employed workers are:

Administrators (education & related fields) 13,000
Managers, (property & real estate) 87,000
Funeral directors 10,000
Managers & administrators............................. 840,000
Management-related occupations 231,000

(Under the heading of management-related occupations the following dominate: accountants and auditors (98,000), underwriters and other financial officers (33,000), management analysts (45,000), wholesale and retail trade buyers (19,000) and business and promotion agents (18,000.)

Architects 21,000
Engineers 34,000
Mathematical and computer scientists 11,000
Natural scientists 17,000
(Of these the vast majority are geologists and geodesists, of which there are 10,000 self-employed.)
Physicians... 134,000
Dentists 80,000

(Dentistry is one of the most self-employed of all professions, with 63% of all dentists being self-employed. This in contrast to a quarter of all physicians and just over half of all veterinarians. Doctors have incorporated at such a rate that there are less than half as many self-employed doctors today as there were in 1970. This flies in the face of the mythology which says that a large number of the self-employed are medical doctors.)

Veterinarians 19,000
Optometrists 12,000
Registered nurses 16,000
Pharmacists 13,000
Therapists 11,000
Psychologists 27,000
Clergy 28,000
Lawyers 210,000
            (This constitutes 34 percent of the total.)
Authors 47,000
Designers 91,000
Musicians and composers 71,000
Actors and directors 10,000
Painters, sculptors, craft artists and art printmakers 98,000
Photographers 43,000
Artists, performers, related workers, NEC 18,000
Editors and reporters 13,000
Public relations specialists 10,000
Teachers, NEC 129,000

(NEC stands for "not elsewhere classified," and in the case of
teachers it refers to teachers outside normal institutional settings
ranging from golf pros to private music teachers. Other than these
there are virtually no self-employed teachers except for the 8,000
prekindergarten and kindergarten teachers.)

Technical, Sales and Administrative Support

2,114,000, which is only about six percent of the total employed in these
occupations.

Computer programmers 17,000

(By far, the leading freelance occupation in the technical support
occupations. There are, on the other hand, more than 1.8 million
self-employed in the sales occupations including these with more than
10,000 apiece.)

Sales supervisors and proprietors 761,000
Insurance sales 120,000
Real estate sales 207,000
Securities and financial services sales 35,000
Sales occupations, other business services 31,000
Commodities sales reps (not retail) 136,000
Sales workers (motor vehicles and boats) 18,000
Sales workers (apparel) 19,000

Sales workers (furniture and home furnishings) 17,000
Sales workers (radio, TV, hifi appliances) 12,000
Sales workers (other commodities) 96,000
Sales counter clerks 12,000
Cashiers 29,000
Street and door-to-door sales workers 212,000
News vendors 59,000

(One small but traditionally self-employed sales position remains that way: most of the nation's 7,000 auctioneers are self-employed.)

Secretaries 32,000
Stenographers 12,000
Typists 16,000
Information clerk 19,000
Bookkeepers, accounting and auditing clerks 122,000
Adjusters and investigators 10,000

Service Occupations

887,000, which is less than 6% of the total number of almost 14 million Americans in this category. These occupations dominate with 10,000 or more self-employed.

887,000, which is less than 6% of the total number of almost 14 million Americans in this category. These occupations dominate with 10,000 or more self-employed.

Bartenders 26,000
Cooks 51,000
Nursing aides, orderlies and attendants 10,000
Maids and housemen 18,000
Janitors and cleaners 71,000
Barbers 60,000
Hairdressers and cosmetologists 254,000
Child-care workers 336,000
Personal Service Occupations, NEC 16,000

Precision Production, Craft and Repair

1,527,000 or some 12% of the total. The dominant self-employed occupations are:

Automobile mechanics 161,000
Bus, truck and stationary engine mechanics 16,000
Small-engine repairers 12,000

Auto body and related repairers 53,000
Industrial machinery repairers 17,000
Electrical and electronic equipment repairers 43,000
Heating, air-conditioning, refrigeration mechanics 33,000
Camera, watch and musical instrument repairers 20,000
Mechanics and repairers, NEC 35,000
Supervisors (construction occupations) 88,000
Brickmasons and stonemasons 47,000
Tile setters (hard and soft) 11,000
Carpet installers 36,000
Carpenters 331,000
Drywall installers 21,000
Electricians 46,000
Painters 152,000
Paperhangers 15,000
Plumbers, pipefitters and steamfitters 51,000
Paving (surfacing and tamping) 30,000
Construction trades, NEC 20,000
Precious stones and metals workers 15,000
Cabinetworkers and bench carpenters 17,000
Furniture and wood finishers 13,000
Dressmakers 50,000
Upholsterers 28,000
Shoe repairers 12,000
Dental laboratory and medical appliance technicians 13,000
Bakers 12,000

Operators, Fabricators and Laborers

599,000, which is a mere 3.7% of the total. The only occupations
with more than 10,000 workers are:

Printing machine operators 10,000
Textile sewing machine operators 12,000
Laundry and dry cleaning machine operators 11,000
Welders and cutters 27,000
Assemblers 19,000
Hand printing, coating and decorating occupations 15,000
Miscellaneous hand working occupations 18,000

Transportation and Material Moving Occupations

344,000, or 8% of the national total. The areas in which there are
more than 10,000 individuals are:

Truck drivers (heavy) 219,000
Truck driver (light) 19,000
Taxi cab drivers and chauffeurs......................... 16,000
Drivers-sales workers................................. 39,000
Excavating and loading machine operators................ 17,000
Grader, dozer and scraper and operators 10,000

Handlers, Equipment Cleaners, Helpers and Laborers

74,000. Numerically not a very important category because the percentage of self-employed is quite low (1.7%). The largest number is in the general category of "Laborers, except construction," where there are a mere 35,000 self-employed workers out of a total of over a million.

Farming, Forestry and Fishing

1,580,000 or 42% of the 3,700,000 Americans in this area. The vast majority of these are farmers. There are 1,369,000 farmers in the United States, of which 1,314,000 or 96% are self-employed. In addition, the following occupations in this area had 10,000 or more self-employed.

Farm workers 29,000
Agricultural supervisors 24,000
Groundskeepers and gardeners (non-farm) 113,000
Timber cutting and logging 30,000
Fishers 30,000

In 1983 there were still a few thousand professional hunters and trappers, all self-employed.

It is worth noting that a vast number of professions contain virtually no self-employed people and rate a zero in the BLS printout (a zero means that there are fewer than 500, but in many cases a zero represents a number closer to a true zero). Besides such obvious areas as the armed forces and employees of labor unions, some of these professions include: nuclear engineers, actuaries, statisticians, chemists, atmospheric and space scientists, college and university teachers, archivists, sociologists, elevator operators, aircraft mechanics, elevator installers and repairers, boilermakers, apparel and fabric patternmakers, bookbinders, shoe machine operators, parking lot attendants, marine engineers, stevedores, and graders and sorters of agricultural products.

5. How do these break down in terms of age and sex?

The breakdown for the year 1983 is as follows based on Bureau of Labor Statistics information:

Age	Total Self-employed	Men	Women
16 to 19	127,000	94,000	33,000
20 to 24	224,000	104,000	120,000
25 to 34	2,183,000	1,509,000	674,000
35 to 44	2,261,000	1,562,000	698,000
45 to 54	1,819,000	1,283,000	536,000
55 to 64	1,525,000	1,131,000	394,000
65 & over	790,000	597,000	194,000
Total all ages	9,140,000	6,491,000	2,649,000

(Note: These figures are usually broken down into agricultural and non-agricultural categories by the BLS; however, they have been combined here.)

Several interesting things can be discovered when these statistics are compared to others, namely:

• that while the percentage of self-employed who are women is 29%, this represents a remarkable increase:

Year	Self-employed Women	Percentage of self-employed
1950	1.0 million	11%
1965	1.6 million	18%
1980	2.2 million	26%
1983	2.6 million	29%

If the pattern were to continue in the future, it would look like this:

1995	3.4 million	40%
2010	4.7 million	55%

Another way of looking at the rise of the self-employed woman is to realize their numbers increased by 10% between 1980 to 1982 while

APPENDIX   137

the number of self-employed men went up only 1% during the same period. Just as dramatic is a figure developed by the Small Business Administration which showed that between 1977 and 1980 the number of female sole proprietorships jumped by 33% while the number of female wage and salary workers went up only 14%.

Any way that one looks at it, women have made an unprecedented move into self-employed professions. Compare this to a 1975 Social Security Administration report which lamented the fact that women in the United States have "rarely" become self-employed. An interesting final comment on this phenomenon was made in the July 1984 *Monthly Labor Review* by Eugene H. Becker: "To the extent that the total female labor force is growing more rapidly than the male labor force, the increase in self-employed women is to be expected. Nevertheless, the continued increase in the number of self-employed women may also indicate an expansion in the employment opportunities women are creating for themselves."

• that the self-employed are becoming younger. Compare these percentages:

Year	16-24 years	25-44 years	45 years and older
1972	5.4%	35.8%	58.8%
1979	6.6%	45.3%	49.1%
1983	6.0%	48.6%	45.2%

This is especially remarkable and significant because of the fact that the population at large is becoming older. It must rank as one of the few areas in which the population is not "graying." Nor is this the only study to find this. A Small Business Administration study of self-employment between 1960 and 1975 found the average age holding at 49 years for the years 1961 through 1970, dropping to 48 for the next two years and then to 47 in the 1973-75 period. Analysts at the BLS have found that women tend to become self-employed at a slightly younger age, which has had some bearing on this, but it is not the only factor.

Even more dramatic is the fact that earlier studies of the self-employed described them as noticeably aging and aged. For instance, a study by the Social Security Administration of self-employment in the 1960-65 period concluded: "Self-employed persons are substantially older than persons in wage and salary employment—the difference in median ages was not less than 12 years in 1960, 1963 or 1965." To quote another study of that period, Joseph Phillips' *The Self-Employed in the United States,* this was in part "due to discrimination by employers against older workers." Phillips concluded that this was a population increasingly populated by "older people cut off from the main stream." All of this points to the unavoidable conclusion that this has changed. The turnabout in self-employment is not just that there are more people involved but that they are younger and not accepting self-employment as a consequence of corporate age discrimination.

• that self-employed people work longer and retire later than their salaried counterparts. While only 9% of the workforce is self-employed, a disproportionate number—38%—of those working past 65 are self-employed. What's more, the proportion of the self-employed who are working past 65 years is going up. In 1980, for instance, the self-employed comprised 27.2% of the workforce over 65. This point bears directly on the Social Security debate in that the self-employed who pay more than the conventionally employed also postpone taking their benefits for much longer. This shows they also pay self-employment taxes for a longer period than the employed.

6.   How many hours per week are self-employed people working on the average, is it rising or falling and how does it compare to the hours worked by wage and salary workers?

The assumption has always been that self-employed people work considerably longer than others. It would appear that this has been true but is becoming less so. This can be best shown by the use of this graph showing non-agricultural self-employed *vs.* wage and salary workers.

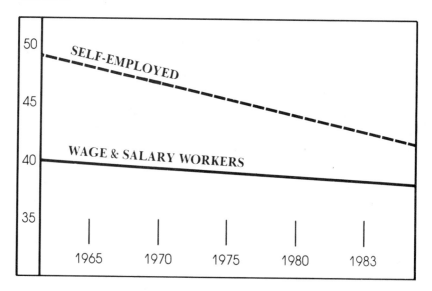

This does nothing to support the "workaholic" notion of self-employment. Not only are self-employed people working fewer hours, but if present trends are projected into the future, they will be working the same number of hours as everyone else before long and, if you believe in straight line projections, fewer hours after that. It is not an insignificant fact that as of 1983 the average length of a workweek for a self-employed American was exactly 40.0 hours. This is only 2.1 hours more than that for employed workers and much less than, say, 1971 when the difference was 9.1 hours. As for farm work, the difference was much greater. In 1983, self-employed farmers worked 47.4 while wage and salary agricultural workers put in an average of 40.3 hours.

It is interesting to note that self-employed women—like women working for wages and salaries—work a shorter week than men, according to the 1983 statistics. Self-employed, non-agricultural women worked 33.4 hours while men in the same position worked 43.0 hours. For wage and salary workers women worked 34.5 hours on average and men worked 40.8. That self-employed women work a shorter average week is understandable since that option may have been a major factor in drawing them to self-employment, especially those with small children.

Also noteworthy is the fact that the self-employed work a slightly longer amount of time during the year. These figures from 1982 show this:

Weeks worked	Percentage of self-employed (including agriculture)	Percentage of wage and salary workers
1-13 Weeks	6.1	9.6
14-26 Weeks	8.4	9.4
27-39 Weeks	6.2	8.3
40-49 Weeks	10.0	9.7
50-52 Weeks	69.2	63.0

7. **Where are self-employed people most likely to be found and what are the states where the rise in self-employment is most dramatic?**

Based on the results of the 1980 Census, the greatest number was to be found in California, followed by Texas, New York, Illinois,

Pennsylvania and Florida, in that order. Here are the numbers for all the states and the District of Columbia:

Alabama	101,432	Montana	38,645
Alaska	12,362	Nebraska	92,388
Arizona	64,653	Nevada	22,040
Arkansas	85,735	New Hampshire	29,396
California	803,909	New Jersey	158,628
Colorado	110,668	New Mexico	37,620
Connecticut	74,555	New York	402,160
Delaware	12,796	North Carolina	181,783
D.C.	11,104	North Dakota	46,264
Florida	275,690	Ohio	246,735
Georgia	147,001	Oklahoma	126,537
Hawaii	23,388	Oregon	102,921
Idaho	45,661	Pennsylvania	292,178
Illinois	292,254	Rhode Island	19,495
Indiana	138,277	South Carolina	77,779
Iowa	150,356	South Dakota	51,184
Kansas	108,905	Tennessee	136,611
Kentucky	106,657	Texas	483,982
Louisiana	104,617	Utah	39,774
Maine	38,133	Vermont	21,688
Maryland	91,061	Virginia	124,498
Massachusetts	127,346	Washington	130,466
Michigan	187,536	West Virginia	39,922
Minnesota	183,037	Wisconsin	147,892
Mississippi	74,040	Wyoming	16,962
Missouri	182,079		

These figures are based on the 1980 Census total of 6,617,700 self-employed, which falls 1,861,000 short of the BLS total for 1980. This discrepancy aside, it does give a good idea of the distribution of the self-employed in the United States.

When coupled with the figures on the annual rates at which self-employment has grown in each state one can get an even better idea of the situation state by state. These are figures from the Bureau of Economic Analysis of the Commerce Department based on tax returns (Form 1040 Schedule SE).

Annual Percentage Change in Employment by Class of Worker by State: 1970-1980

State	Total Employment	Wage/Salary	Self-Employment
Alabama	2.23	2.32	1.49
Alaska	5.02	4.83	7.73*
Arizona	6.53	6.62	0.55
Arkansas	2.68	2.99	1.21
California	3.78	3.69	4.90*
Colorado	5.36	5.54	3.94
Connecticut	1.87	1.82	2.50*
Delaware	1.43	1.45	1.01
D.C.	0.19	0.17	0.90
Florida	5.28	5.34	4.61
Georgia	2.78	2.90	1.71
Hawaii	3.24	2.90	4.82*
Idaho	4.16	4.71	1.79
Illinois	0.75	0.75	0.38
Indiana	1.41	0.75	0.78
Iowa	1.71	2.26	0.35
Kansas	2.65	3.15	0.37
Kentucky	2.01	2.33	0.49
Louisiana	3.37	3.60	1.22
Maine	2.17	2.11	2.64*
Maryland	2.15	2.16	2.10
Massachusetts	1.44	1.41	1.87*
Michigan	1.12	1.15	0.75
Minnesota	3.04	3.39	0.99
Mississippi	2.03	2.51	-0.35
Missouri	1.25	1.37	0.50
Montana	3.00	3.32	1.66
Nebraska	2.29	2.72	0.52
Nevada	8.40	8.60	5.68
New Hampshire	4.03	3.96	4.77*
New Jersey	1.33	1.32	1.51*
New Mexico	4.57	4.78	2.73
New York	-0.05	-0.08	0.31*
North Carolina	2.12	2.45	-0.19
North Dakota	2.53	3.54	-0.22
Ohio	0.85	0.85	0.85
Oklahoma	3.36	3.85	0.97
Oregon	4.17	4.20	3.91
Pennsylvania	0.70	0.69	0.84*
Rhode Island	0.89	0.82	2.04*

State	Total Employment	Wage/Salary	Self-Employment
South Carolina	2.73	2.90	1.21
South Dakota	1.16	0.44	-0.54
Tennessee	2.48	2.78	0.66
Texas	4.47	4.78	2.11
Utah	4.66	4.72	4.11
Vermont	2.30	2.19	3.20
Virginia	2.84	3.00	1.27
Washington	3.82	3.86	3.46
West Virginia	1.72	1.87	0.49
Wisconsin	2.20	2.46	0.45
Wyoming	6.97	7.61	3.26
US TOTAL	2.23	2.32	1.49

(An asterisk indicates that the annual percentage increase in self-employment exceeded that of wage and salary employees during the decade.)

8. To what extent has self-employment become a force in the economy of the 1980s?

What is most dramatic are the changes which took place between 1980 and 1982 during which time wage and salary employment fell 0.7% but non-farm self-employment rose 4.3%. Roughly speaking, this represented a period of recession and underscores the importance of the self-employment option during such periods. As presented by the Small Business Administration in its 1983 annual report, here is what happened, organized by SBA regions:

	SELF-EMPLOYMENT				
	Wage & salary	Farm	Non-farm	Total	Total change
Region I, Total	-0.5	-5.0	4.0	3.3	-0.3
Connecticut	0.1	2.3	3.8	3.7	-0.2
Maine	-1.2	-5.2	3.8	2.3	-0.8
Massachusetts	-0.8	-11.0	4.3	3.8	-0.5
New Hampshire	2.2	-6.1	3.7	2.7	2.3
Rhode Island	-2.6	-13.7	3.8	3.1	-2.2
Vermont	0.4	-2.8	3.4	1.8	0.6

	SELF-EMPLOYMENT				
	Wage & salary	Farm	Non-farm	Total	Total change
Region II, Total	0.3	3.7	4.4	4.3	0.5
New Jersey	-0.2	0.8	4.1	4.0	0.1
New York	0.5	4.2	4.5	4.5	0.7
Region III, Total	-2.2	0.5	3.8	3.1	-1.8
Delaware	-0.2	-3.4	3.9	2.3	0.0
D.C.	-3.7	0.0	8.0	8.0	-3.4
Maryland	-1.1	2.7	4.3	4.1	-0.8
Pennsylvania	-3.4	-3.4	3.5	2.4	-2.9
Virginia	0.7	3.2	3.7	3.6	0.9
West Virginia	-6.4	3.0	3.0	3.0	-5.5
Region IV, Total	0.5	-2.3	3.1	1.2	0.5
Alabama	-2.2	-1.8	1.5	0.1	-1.9
Florida	4.8	5.1	4.6	4.7	4.8
Georgia	2.8	-1.9	2.5	1.1	2.7
Kentucky	-2.9	-1.0	3.2	1.0	-2.3
Mississippi	-4.0	-3.8	1.9	-0.8	-3.6
North Carolina	-0.1	-5.7	2.6	-0.5	-0.1
South Carolina	-0.8	-5.9	2.4	-0.4	-0.8
Tennessee	-3.3	-1.1	2.9	1.1	-2.8
Region V, Total	-4.9	-1.4	4.4	2.5	-4.2
Illinois	-3.8	3.0	5.3	3.0	-3.3
Indiana	-5.1	0.9	4.0	2.9	-4.2
Michigan	-6.5	-1.6	3.8	2.4	-5.8
Minnesota	-4.0	-1.1	4.6	2.0	-3.2
Ohio	-5.7	-2.2	4.1	2.4	-5.0
Wisconsin	-3.4	-1.3	4.4	2.2	-2.8
Region VI, Total	5.1	-1.1	4.2	2.4	4.8
Arkansas	-3.6	-3.7	2.4	-0.4	-3.1
Louisiana	2.3	1.2	3.7	3.0	2.3
New Mexico	2.5	-0.3	4.6	3.3	2.5
Oklahoma	7.1	-1.5	4.7	2.0	6.4
Texas	6.8	-0.7	4.4	2.9	6.4
Region VII, Total	-2.9	-1.9	4.6	1.5	-2.2
Iowa	-6.1	-2.0	4.5	1.0	-4.8
Kansas	-0.8	1.1	5.1	3.3	-0.2

| | SELF-EMPLOYMENT | | | | |
	Wage & salary	Farm	Non-farm	Total	Total change
Missouri	-2.1	-2.7	4.5	1.4	-1.6
Nebraska	-2.9	-3.6	4.5	0.4	-2.4
Region VIII, Total	3.8	-3.0	4.9	2.1	3.6
Colorado	8.2	-2.3	5.2	3.8	-7.7
Montana	-1.7	0.1	4.6	2.9	-0.9
North Dakota	-2.0	-5.0	4.9	-1.3	1.3
South Dakota	-3.3	-4.2	4.5	-0.4	-2.7
Utah	1.4	-1.0	4.5	3.2	1.6
Wyoming	2.1	-0.5	5.6	3.8	2.3
Region IX, Total	0.4	-0.1	6.0	5.5	0.9
Arizona	1.2	2.5	5.8	5.5	1.5
California	0.4	-0.3	6.1	5.5	0.8
Hawaii	-0.4	-0.5	6.4	5.5	-0.0
Nevada	0.5	-0.6	5.1	4.7	0.8
Region X, Total	-3.1	1.8	4.1	3.5	-2.3
Alaska	14.4	10.8	5.1	5.2	13.6
Idaho	-4.5	-0.8	3.7	1.9	-3.5
Oregon	-7.8	2.7	4.0	3.7	-6.4
Washington	-1.8	2.4	4.2	3.8	-1.3
United States	-0.7	-1.3	4.3	2.7	-0.3

Another way of looking at this 1980-82 period is to note the extent to which smaller businesses provided jobs while the larger firms did not. Between 1980 and 1982 employment in the United States rose by 1.9% overall, but it fell for companies with more than 500 employees while smaller enterprises all posted gains:

—Firms with 1-19 employees .... up 9.0% from 16.4 million to 17.8 million
—Firms with 20-99 employees .... up 3.9% from 13.9 million to 14.4 million
—Firms with 100-499 employees .... up 4.3% from 12.4 million to 13.0 million
—Firms with more than 500 employees ...down 1.6% from 50.3 million to 49.5 million

Still another way to look at this is in terms of the impact of the income of the self-employed on the economy of a state or a region. The Small Business Administration noted in its 1984 edition of *The State of Small Business* that sole proprietorship income can "have a significant impact in raising a state's overall level of income." For instance, in the second quarter of 1983 such income was 7.3% of earned personal income for the nation at large, but was 22.3% of earned personal income in South Dakota, 13.2% in Kansas and 12.4% in Idaho. This is added evidence that self-employment has growing power as a positive force in the economy and was a documentable factor in pulling the nation out of its last recession.

9. What else do we know about these people?

What remains are odd facts and trends which help complete the statistical portrait. In no special order we have the following.

- *Income.* In his article "Self-Employed Workers: An Update to 1983" Eugene H. Becker says, "Persons who work for themselves continue to earn less than their wage and salary counterparts. Despite a generally longer work week, self-employed persons in 1982 earned, on average, only about 70% as much as wage and salary workers, that is $12,595 compared with $17,559." Becker is quick to point out that there are a number of professions in which self-employment was more remunerative than wage and salary work.

- *Time in Job.* Generally speaking, men have been at self-employed work for a longer period than wage and salary men have been with their current employers. Self-employed women, not in agriculture, have not been on their own for quite as long as their employed counterparts. This seems completely consistent with the fact that many self-employed women are recent arrivals.

The latest statistics on this are BLS figures from January 1983:

Median Years with Current Employer for workers 25 Years and Over

	Total	Men	Women
Agriculture			
Wage and salary workers	4.5	4.8	3.1
Self-employed	17.3	19.0	10.4
Nonagricultural			
Wage and salary workers	5.6	6.6	4.8
Self-employed	6.4	7.5	4.4

• *Failure Rates.* In 1983 Thomas A. Gray and David A. Hirschberg of the Small Business Administration studied the self-employed (representing "the smallest of small businesses") to see how they maintained self-employment over a five-year period. Using samples in two periods, 1960-64 and 1970-74, they found that about half survived the five years as self-employed workers albeit sometimes shifting to a different industry as a self-employed worker. Here are the findings for the two periods studied:

Self-Employed 1960–64 and 1970–74 as a Percentage of 1960 and 1970 Self-Employed

	1960	1961	1962	1963	1964	1970	1971	1972	1973	1974
Self-employed same industry		65.7	57.9	51.9	46.8		43.7	37.7	33.9	30.0
Self-employed different industry		5.5	6.7	7.3	8.1		23.9	22.4	23.2	22.0
Total	100	71.2	64.6	59.2	54.9	100	67.6	60.1	57.1	52.0

The bulk of these self-employed from both periods took wage and salary jobs (about 18%), or ended up in a partially employed and partially self-employed status (about 7%) or ended up "not employed" (about 20%). "Not employed" is defined as those out of work, retired or working but outside the Social Security System (such as Federal employees who are out of the system and are, ironically, deemed "not employed" by government economists).

One curiosity is that in the figures from the 1970s, a large percentage changed their form of self-employment. Those who developed the figures report, "There is no immediate explanation for this anomaly." The immediate conclusion made by Gray and Hirschberg is that "if an individual self-employed in one year survives as self-employed through year two there is a high probability that individual will maintain self-employment over time." When you take retirement and people who are employed part time into account, the failure rate is relatively low and nothing like those oft-heard lines about nine out of ten small businesses—and by implication the self-employed—failing in short order.

This study also concluded that the "failures" who went back to regular employment tended to make more money than average and that those who were both self-employed and employed made the most money. It was also found that the increase in earnings for those who stuck with self-employment for each of the periods outstripped the increase for the employed. In other words, self-employed income tends to rise at a greater rate than wage and salary income.

- *Self-Employed Blacks* Historically, blacks have had a minimal share in self-employment and have tended to generate significantly lower earnings than their white counterparts. Even during the period from 1960 to 1970 when there was a major move up the occupational scale by black workers, there was only a modest increase in black self-employment. A study by the Social Security Administration revealed a mere rise of 3,000 black self-employed during the 1960s. Their percentage of the total went from a scant 1.9% of self-employment to a skimpy 2.2% between 1960 and 1970.

The picture began to change in the 1970s; their number grew by nearly 60,000 between 1972 and 1979, giving them a 5.5% share. Blacks were still underrepresented, but less so. Also, according to the Bureau of Labor Statistics, the black self-employed tended to gravitate to blue-collar and service occupations while whites were more likely to enter higher paying white-collar occupations.

However, since then the number has fallen by 100,000 and the percentage of the self-employed workforce which is black has dropped from a stable 5.5% in 1979 to 3.8% in 1983. The Bureau of Labor Statistics, which came up with the figures, had no immediate explanation for the drop-off. During the same period, however, the number of blacks with wage and salary jobs increased by 30%.

Ironically, at about the same time that the BLS discovery was made, the 1984 annual report of the Small Business Administration was released. It contained a special appendix on the rise of minority-owned business which looked at the period from 1972 through 1982 and concluded that non-white self-employment had jumped by 43% while white self-employment had gone up 35%. It also reported that self-employment was attracting younger, better educated numbers of minority groups. The vast majority of the minority self-employed (85%) were in the general areas of service, retail trade and construction.

As this study was about all minorities it is significant that blacks ranked last when it came to the likelihood of becoming self-employed. The "likelihood" ranking was: (1) white, (2) Asian, (3) Hispanic and (4) black.

It is clear that there have been moderate gains for blacks in self-employment, but that they are still very much underrepresented. Despite its attempt to be upbeat about minority self-employment, the SBA report said, "Blacks and other selected minority groups, including Hispanics, often face significant impediments to business entry that range from low family income and inadequate occupational training to differences in educational attainment."

10. Enough about the legitimate self-employed who are part of the statistics—what about that part of the "underground economy" which is made up of self-employed?

There have been several attempts to estimate the number of self-employed who are part of the underground economy and are totally "off the books." The estimates which are most often cited range widely and usually don't distinguish between those in standard occupations and those who smuggle drugs, pimp or run numbers.

However, a 1981 study by the General Accounting Office concentrated only on legal self-employment and concluded that there were 1,500,000 self-employed who paid neither taxes nor Social Security payments on their self-employment. About half of these people filed some form of return, such as wage and salary income, meaning that half of them moonlighted in unreported self-employed jobs. This finding would tend to agree with a Census study released in 1973 concluding that 700,000 full-time self-employed undergrounders came into the economy between the 1950s and 1981. Based on these two studies, a total of 750,000 full-time self-employed in legal occupations seems about right.

Of the total 1.5 million in the GAO study, it was determined that approximately one in four worked in agricultural production and that one in four was over 65 years of age. The largest percentage was in the South (37.1%) and the smallest percentage in the Northeast (16.1%).

According to this survey, the top ten occupations for self-employed tax avoiders are:

1. Farmers—446,000
2. Managers and Administrators—183,000
3. Child-care workers (excluding private household)—68,000
4. Restaurant, cafeteria and bar managers—48,000
5. Carpenters—46,000
6. Painters, construction and maintenance—44,000
7. Newsboys—43,000 (an estimated 71% do not report.)
8. Automobile mechanics—31,000
9. Hairdressers and cosmetologists—27,000
10. Gardeners and groundskeepers—25,000

These were followed by sales clerks, dressmakers, truck drivers, teachers, registered nurses, insurance agents, brokers and underwriters; real estate agents and brokers; bookkeepers; plumbers and pipe fitters; demonstrators (sales); janitors and sextons; sales reps (wholesale trade); child-care workers (private household); roofers and slaters; and brick and stone masons.

Predictably, the cost of this is tremendous. The GAO study estimated that in 1976 the amount lost in Social Security taxes alone from the self-employed was $1.06 billion. Bear in mind that this did not include those self-employed who underreported income. The IRS estimated that for that same year some 3.1 million self-employed underreported income (as opposed to 600,000 self-employed who overreported income).

One conclusion from this is that the "aboveground" self-employed suffer the consequence of the reputation that a lot of us are beating the system. Dating back to the Congressional hearings of the 1950s which explored the original Keogh plan, a common belief expressed by those opposing the rights of the self-employed is that they should not be given those rights because so many of them cheat. And even though there is evidence that as more wage and salary workers find a way to participate in the underground economy (more than twice as many, according to the Census Bureau study), the impression is that it is much harder—if not impossible—for them to do so because their taxes are withheld. This is not so and has been shown not to be so in the various studies of the underground economy; but the impression remains.

COMING TO TERMS

A Somewhat Irreverent Glossary for Thinking about Self-employment and Employment

Almost every type of work has its own set of terms; yet self-employment has been curiously lacking in this regard. Here are some terms gathered from many sources which apply to the self-employed. For contrast, the list also includes some of the vogue words (sometimes impertinently defined) which are now in use where people are employed by others.

Besides working as a glossary, it is hoped that the list also serves as a quick run through the major concepts which people planning their working future can play with. For what it is worth, many of these terms are those which I use in thinking about work.

Ad-hocracy   Term created by Alvin Toffler in *Future Shock* to describe a system of work in which teams accomplish a job on an ad hoc basis. Toffler believes that the ad-hocracy is the organization of the future which will ultimately supplement the bureaucracy. Some self-employed workers are already ad-hocratic in the sense that they can drift in and out of work for an organization on a contract basis as consultants, specialists or whatever.

Alternative Profession   Term introduced in the 1970s to cover a group of odd new professions which people were creating, ranging from those who delivered birthday greetings dressed as gorillas to those who would come in and help you rearrange your closets. Some, like chimney sweeping, were revivals of old professions while others were whimsical variations on traditional services, such as the many odd "-grams" (balloongrams, strip-o-grams, etc.) offered as an alternative to the plain old telegram. Some amount to little more than "gofer" services in which chores and errands are run for fees in the neighborhood of $20 an hour. If nothing else they tend to be well named: Chores Truly, Rent-a-Yenta, Irons-in-the-Fire, etc.

At the outset, these oddball businesses were considered by many to be a short-lived phenomenon but they have, if anything, become more popular. An article in the *Christian Science Monitor* for October 12, 1973 said, "Some vocational analysts contend that what they see as the 'alternative employment fad' will go the way of the hula-hoop." However, these alternative professions have proliferated for a number of reasons including the fact that they require little capital to start. They have become a haven for the self-employed.

Anomie   Defined in the 1973 HEW study *Work in America* as "a condition of deracination—a feeling of rootlessness, lifelessness and dissociation—a word which in the original Greek meant a string that does not vibrate, that has lost its vitality." It has been seen as the condition which afflicts those without work or those with meaningless or marginal work.

Bad Debt   Receivables which you cannot collect. Self-employed people learn to budget a percentage of their estimated income for bad debts.

Behavior Modification   According to *Behavior Improvement News*, it is "the technology of human resource development."

Benefit Shock   The shock which comes to those who leave large organizations with liberal benefit packages to become self-employed. The shock comes when the person fully realizes that there is nobody around to provide these benefits and that they will have to be purchased on the open market (e.g. health insurance) or forgotten about (e.g. paid holidays).

Benevolent Capitalist   Term, as used in a *Washington Post* article entitled "Yesteryear's Hippie Is Today's Capitalist," to describe those former counterculturalists who now have their own businesses. As implied, these businesses tend to be in areas like solar energy, natural food and cabinetmaking rather than, say, stripmining.

"Bermuda Triangle"   According to the December 29, 1981 *Wall Street Journal*, this is a term which has been applied to the administrator of the Small Business Administration because, as one

SBA official put it, "when something goes in, it never comes out." For the self-employed the term is occasionally applicable to state licensing authorities, zoning boards and other organizations with which they must deal.

Between Jobs   Out of work.

The Blues   Pejorative catchall for Blue Cross and Blue Shield, usually applied after the rates have gone up.

Breakout   Current term for a deviation from a master management-labor agreement such as those which have been adopted in which workers have agreed to lower wages to keep a company from going out of business. Self-employed people create "breakouts" all the time.

Burnout   Job-related malady characterized by such symptoms as apathy, frustration, cynicism, absenteeism and alcohol dependency.

Cafeteria Plan   Name for flexible benefit package offered by some companies under which employees can apply credits to combinations of benefits. At the American Can Co., for example, new hires get a shopping list of benefits to choose from in setting up their benefit plans. It is not unlike the shopping for benefits that the self-employed must engage in except for the fact that the self-employed must pay for them out of pocket.

Cohort   Demographic term for a group of people naturally associated, such as the baby-boom cohort or the cohort of Vietnam veterans. It is an appropriate term for the self-employed who are a cohort with common interests and motivations but diverse occupations.

Cola   Acronym for Cost of Living Adjustment, something written into some employment contracts. Self-employed people generally fall into the UNCOLA category (Unable to Negotiate Cost of Living Adjustments).

Commuter   A person who moves an average of 18 miles to and from work each day. Here are two much better definitions: "A man who shaves and takes a train. And then rides back to shave again"—E.B. White. "A commuter is one who never knows how a show comes out because he has to leave early to catch a train to get him back to the country in time to catch a train to bring him back to the city"—Ogden Nash.

Corporate Culture   The business buzzword of the 1980s, according to the *New York Times*. (It fills the shoes that "decentralization" filled in the 1960s and "corporate strategy" did in the 1970s.) It refers to an organization's climate, feeling, rituals, mythology and other qualities that don't show in the black and white of the annual report. The idea that the culture of a corporation is the real key to its performance is advocated in *In Search of Excellence* by Thomas J. Peters and Robert H. Waterman, Jr. and in *Corporate Cultures: The Rites and Rituals of Corporate Life* by Terence E. Deal and Allen A. Kennedy.

Corporation   Classically defined by Supreme Court Justice John Marshall in 1819 as "an artificial being, invisible, intangible, and existing only in contemplation of law." A continuing debate which the self-employed have with themselves is whether or not to become a "private corporation."

Cottage Industry   Home-based production. The term is getting a new workout as the practice of working at home increases—both with and without the benefit of electronics. It has been given new status with the current assertion that many of the nation's new computer software companies started as cottage industries. The concept is also at the center of the debate over the legality of working out of your home.
    Although the practice has been around since the Middle Ages, the term, according to a 1984 article in *Rural America*, only dates back to 1921 when it first showed up in a British publication. (See also "Electronic Cottage" and "Fair Labor Standards Act.")

"Crown Prince Syndrome"   Describing the tendency on the part of some corporations to focus their greatest attention on those employees who will make it to the top.

Cyberphobia   Fear or hatred of computers which has advanced to the point where the person cannot function normally. Professor Sanford Weinberg of St. Joseph's University, who claims to have coined the term, points to a policeman who shot a computer console as an example of one suffering from this malady. Weinberg has also studied cyberphilia, present in those who are so hooked on computers that they cannot get along with humans.

Cyclical Self-employment   Term used by the Bureau of Labor Statistics, among others, to describe the tendency for self-employment to rise and fall with bad economic times. The theory, which was demonstrated graphically in the 1980-82 recession, is that the rate of self-employment rises faster in bad times when traditional jobs are harder to find.

De-maturity   The central concept in the book *Industrial Renaissance* by William J. Abernathy, Kim B. Clark and Alan M. Kantrow. Maturity in this case refers to companies which become so dominated by a production method or technology that they cannot change quickly enough when the market demands change. "De-maturity" refers to those who are committed to innovation, flexibility and diversity.

Discontinuity   Term used by sociologists, futurists and others to describe a radical shift in direction. It aptly describes the rise in the number of self-employed Americans in recent years and the migration back to rural areas—reversing two of the most important trends which helped define the Industrial Revolution.

"D.P. Theory"   The notion which holds that most entrepreneurs are displaced persons who have been dislodged from an organization. Albert Shapero, who has studied the subject, reported in *Psychology Today* that 65% of the small business owners he surveyed did so because they had been fired, had a promotion blocked or some other bad experience.

Dropout   Name which has been used by the business magazines to describe those who give up demanding business careers to fulfill a personal dream. The term, as used, is misleading. As a *Forbes* cover story entitled "Happy Dropouts," pointed out "...when suddenly cut loose from the corporation or the business they created, these newly liberated dreamers usually throw themselves heart and soul into whatever they do. Do not, therefore, confuse dropping out with being laid back."

   This is in direct contrast to the meaning of the term as it was applied a decade earlier to those who dropped out of organized society.

Dummy Ad   One of the 1980s' worst new concepts. These are want ads trumpeting remarkably good jobs...which don't exist. These abominations are usually placed because a company wants to build a resume file for some future venture which may or may not materialize.

Electronic Cottage   Term coined by futurist Alvin Toffler in his book *The Third Wave* and used as the title of a book by Joseph Deken. Toffler says we are entering the era of the "Electronic cottage"—a return to the old tradition of the cottage industry "on a new, higher, electronic basis with new emphasis on the home as the center of society." The business of information, as such electronically aided work might be called, is vastly superior to the current centralized commuting work situation in terms of energy efficiency, pollution control, and briefly, cost effectiveness.

Electronic Sweatshop   Very unflattering term which some are using to describe the highly touted "Office of the Future" as a throwback to the assembly line in which white-collar workers who used to do many things now do just one in a large factory-like setting. There seems to be evidence to support the sweatshop charge. This paragraph from the May 23, 1983 issue of the *Behavorial Sciences Newsletter* is particularly telling:

> A study by the US Public Health Service compared clerical workers using computer terminals with others doing similar jobs manually. The study found that the clerical workers with the terminals suffered far more physical and mental stress. The reason: They had to follow rigid work procedures and had no control over their work. They were actually controlled by the machine.

The reality of these electronic factories, staffed primarily by women, bids to be a factor as more individuals take a step backward from the "future" and look at old-fashioned independence.

Electronically Extended Family   Phrase used by futurists to describe the potential impact of electronics on the family. Its implication is spelled out in the Institute for the Future's report *Teletext and Videotext in the United States*, "If widespread use of in-home information and communication systems can recreate cottage industries, they might also recreate the extended family. In-home knowledge-related work seems a most suitable form of employment for the elderly."

Emotional Labor   New term for putting your feelings and manners into a job, such as the smiles and chipper attitude which the airlines demand from flight attendants. It is explored critically in the book *The Managed Heart* by Arlie Russell Hochschild.

Entrepreneur   French word for one who undertakes a project and accepts risks, mainly financial. In the study *The Entrepreneur and New Enterprise Formation* the point is made that the only English word which comes close is Daniel DeFoe's word *projector* for one who projects into the future and absorbs the risks of that assertion. In March 1984 the *New York Times* carried a definition of the "new entrepreneur": "A person, usually under 40, independent and imaginative, who starts a business selling a new product or service in the fast-changing American marketplace; most outstanding examples of the species are in high technology, but they also have profited mightily in cookies, clothing, medical services, etc."

Entrepreneurial   A term which is now in vogue in ads for mid-managerial jobs in large corporations. The irony of this application has not been missed. Writing in *Newsweek*, advertising executive Robert W. Hogan remarked, "To describe, say, a product manager's position deep in the honeycomb of some corporate giant as 'entrepreneurial' is somewhat akin to insisting the world is flat; we who've been around know better. A true entrepreneur would last all of five minutes in such a stifling structure."

Ergonomics   Technically, the relationship between humans and the tools and equipment they use. In practice, it refers to the desire to develop and install a machine which won't cause its operator to get a bad back from using it.

The irony of ergonomics becoming, as *The Behavioral Sciences Newsletter* called it in 1982, "a hot new buzzword sweeping the workplace" is that it took until 1982 for this common sense notion to become a "hot new buzzword."

Exclusive Rule   Internal Revenue Service ruling which says that for purposes of tax deductions a home office must only be used for work.

Fair Labor Standards Act (FLSA)   New Deal legislation which effectively outlawed the sweatshop by eliminating child labor and setting minimum wage and hour rules. The act also stipulated that the Department of Labor could outlaw certain types of industrial homework where there were substandard working conditions and wages. The department eventually outlawed work in seven sewing-related areas (knitted outerwear, jewelry, gloves and mittens, buttons and buckles, handkerchiefs, women's apparel and embroidery). All of this became most controversial in recent years as some homeworkers maintained that the rules were a violation of their rights. Meanwhile, organized labor has not only defended the existing bans but began to push to have them extended to telecommuting. The initial bans were lifted in late 1984 by the Department of Labor.

Flexitime   A system which allows workers the freedom to come and go at personally convenient times during the workday. Hundreds of companies and government agencies have discovered that letting employees choose their own hours—within certain limits—not only helps the worker, but also helps the corporation. Self-employed people work under this system as a matter of course. Flexitime has begotten other flex's including *Flexiplace*, the ability to work at home or at a place of employment; *Flexiyear*, the ability to set broad annual patterns; and *Maxi-flex*, which permits people to average 80 hours of work every two weeks to be served any way they like.

Freedom of the Workplace   Phrase which has become the rallying cry behind the drive to lift Federal, state and local bans on working at home. Among other things, it was the name given to a Senate bill, S. 2145, which would lift homework bans created by the Fair Labor Standards Act.

Freelance   The commonest of nicknames for independent work applied to those in fields ranging from consulting to photography.

Some freelancers don't like the term because it implies a willingness to do *anything* presuming the fee is right. Historically, this is so. In his *In Search of History*, Theodore H. White wrote, "A free lance in the waning Middle Ages was a knight without an overlord; free lances were variously horsemen, cavaliers, pikestaff men, who would rent their lances and services to any master per battle or campaign and then go on their way without home, seeking another fee."

Some give it wide berth, preferring such terms as "solo entrepreneur" or "independent contractor."

Genetic Screening   A small but growing number of companies are using this technique on current and prospective employees to determine their susceptibility to work-related disease. A 1983 Congressional study determined that there was much potential for abuse as the practice became more common. One possibility is using the screening to discriminate against people. A company could not discriminate against a black person but might exclude a person prone to sickle cell anemia. Another dark side to the practice would be a company using it to hire only those who are not susceptible to disease and then not worry about the safety of the workplace.

Golden Parachute   Contracts given to executives which guarantee them several years of salary and benefits should they be thrown out after a hostile takeover.

Happy Hour   Described in Thomas M. Camden's *Language Guide to Outplacement* as "A period of time which could be several hours when saloons serve depressants to people who want to escape pressures of work, career, family or self. When was the last time you saw someone really happy and enjoying the 'Happy Hour'?"

Housespouse   Term used in an April 6, 1981 *Washington Post* headline ("Housespouses: Father's Day at School") to cover housewives and househusbands.

H.R.10   The official IRS term for the Keogh pension plan for the self-employed. It was the original House bill number for the legislation, first proposed in the 1950s, and has stayed with it ever since along with Keogh's name.

Industrial Homework   Long-established term for factory work which is done in a person's home. It is a loaded term in the sense that it is a red flag to organized labor, which has historically associated the concept with the exploitation of workers and a part of the "sweating" system.

Information Broker   A good example of a new form of "service economy" job which has been created by self-employed independents. Writing in the May/June 1976 issue of *Special Libraries*, librarian James B. Dodd of the Georgia Institute of Technology had this to say about them, "In the early 1970s there surfaced in the world of libraries and information handling a method of operation that may ultimately have more impact on the profession than its present scope would indicate. This phenomenon is the growing number of independent information brokers who operate primarily as an interface between one or more libraries and paying information users. Their primary purpose is to make a profit."
    It is not clear how many of these operators exist, but it is clear that it is a growing occupation. Some of those who began as independents have developed into small companies. Other terms used to describe information brokers are: independent information specialist, free-lance librarian, information specialist, advocacy librarian and librarian-without-a-library.

Intrapreneur   One who operates as an entrepreneur within bureaucratic system. According to a 1982 article *International Management* magazine, there is now a school in Sweden which trains people to set up small businesses within larger corporations.

Job Security   Along with "postal service" and "military justice" this has been deemed one of the true oxymorons of our time. Organizations which boast that they offer job security are often those which maintain that the rights to fire and layoff are inalienable.

Job Sharing   System by which two people who each wish to work only half a day fill one job. It has proven especially well-suited for teaching and a number of school systems now offer shared jobs. This allows students, women with children and older people who do not want to retire completely to find a place in the working world. It also allows people to work half time for somebody else and the other half for themselves as self-employed workers.

Job War   Term used in the book *The Work Revolution* by Gail Garfield Schwartz and William Neikirk to describe a situation in the not too distant future when a host of factors will create a growing work force fighting for fewer and fewer jobs. The factors include increasing longevity, a rising retirement age and industrial robots and they will produce strife between people of different ages, races and sexes.

Keep-Home Pay   The equivalent of "take-home pay" for the person who works at home. The term was first spotted in an article in the *Washington Post* by George Clifford entitled "The Stay-at-Home Solution to Work." Clifford's point was that greater productivity and higher keep-home pay accrued to those who worked at home.

Labile   See Stabile

Latchkey Children   Used to describe children who come home from school to empty homes where they wait for their parents to come home from work. One of the factors which is often given as a reason for working at home is that it helps a family avoid some of the fears and dangers associated with latchkey situations. Current estimates are that there may be as many as 2 million latchkey kids in the United States between the ages of seven and 13.

Leisure Ethic   The other side of the work ethic defined in the July 15, 1977 issue of *The Behavorial Sciences Newsletter* as a system of values which "says in effect that work is not an absolute, and it can be better to work only as much as you must to support what's really important—leisure activities."

Lone Ranger   Not so long ago this was a deprecatory term for the self-employed in an age of organizations and an ever-growing collection of employee perks. The author of this book would like to see it turned around as a symbol for the wholesale return of the self-employed worker to the American scene. If the connotation of the term were to turn around it would fit with the flip which has taken place with the implied meaning of the next item.

MC-37   Name of the Interstate Commerce Commission order which forbids trucking firms from charging more on shipments to private residents than they do on shipments to commercially zoned locations. It has been heralded as one reform which has helped small home-based business. The authors of the book The New Entrepreneurs, a book about women working out of their homes, point out, "As is always true, the implementation process lags behind the law, and some of the women said they were charged extra for residential deliveries after the Order went into effect."

Middle-Age Misfits   People over 45 who are too young to retire and too old to retrain for new technology. The UN's International Labor Organization has studied them and concluded that there are 500,000,000 of them worldwide and that there will be 700,000,000 of them by the year 2000.

Misemployment   Coined term for people who are working at jobs for which they are not suited. "Misemployment" got a lot of play after the release of a report from the Marketing Survey and Research Corporation in the late 1970s which concluded that 80% of the American workforce may not be suited for the work that they do. For instance, after looking at the sales forces of more than 1,000 companies, it was determined that "55% of all salesmen should not be selling, and that an additional 25%—though qualified to sell-are selling the wrong products in the wrong markets."

Mom and Pop   A couple in business together. The term and the concept have made a comeback in recent years. A 1965 Labor Department publication said that such operations were disappearing as they were "caught up in the swiftly moving tides of change." The tide changed direction as franchise shops, convenience stores, computer services and other new forms of mom and pop operations proliferated. A *USA Today* headline underscored the comeback: "Former Mom and Pop firms soar as programming leaders."

Ironically, the term which used to imply anachronism is now proudly used by those who, as *Money* put it, "enjoy the idea of bumping into each other behind the cash register." Couples so employed often use the term "nooner" when discussing their sex lives.

Mondayish   Defined in *Webster's New International Dictionary* as "Characteristic of Monday, specifically, fagged out after Sunday." Generally speaking, self-employed people don't suffer the Monday malady as often as their employed counterparts as they have the option of working Sunday and sleeping in on Monday.

Networking   Vogueish term for using a series of personal contacts in business. Most self-employed workers have learned to rely on some form of network. Some of these are very informal while others have regular meetings, seminars and newsletters.

OASDI   Short for Old-Age, Survivors and Disability Insurance, which is the proper name for the Social Security system excluding Medicare insurance.

Outlier   One who does not work at home. An admittedly old and obscure term but one which may have increasing usefulness as more and more people work at home and the distinction becomes more common. The nice thing about the term is that is makes those of us who don't commute to work seem like less of an oddity.

Outplacement   Kid glove sacking, usually applied to the firing of management-level employees. Sometimes called "de-hiring," it differs from the old-fashioned sacking in that the company tries to help the person get a new job. In most of the literature on the subject, outplacement is defined as it is in Thomas A. Camden's *Language Guide to Outplacement* as "a benefit provided by an employer...Some have written about it in such glowing terms that it begins to sound like the sacked person is getting the Nobel Prize, but not Jane Bryant Quinn who put it curtly, 'In other words, you're fired.'"

Outplacement Consultant   Person who handles the fired employee for a fee. These consultants provide the fired person with advice, inspiration and the general wherewithal to reapproach the job market. They also advise the person who does the firing—never, for example, fire someone in your own office because you can't leave it and don't fire people on Fridays because it ruins everybody's weekend.

Unheard of just a few years ago, this form of consulting became a $80 million a year industry in the United States during the 1980-82 recession but has subsequently been hurt by recovery. However, according to the November 10, 1982 issue of *USA Today*, sources within the industry predict that it will grow to a $500 million a year business by the end of the century because of such things as technological displacement and the trend of large companies to merge.

Overqualified   Standard employer's excuse for not hiring someone who is too expensive, too old or too well educated.

Own-Account Worker   The specific term which is used to describe self-employment in international labor parlance. The International Labour Organization based in Geneva uses it in its annual *Year Book of*

Labour Statistics to chart self-employment throughout the world. The official definition: "A person who operates his or her own economic enterprise or engages independently in a profession or trade and hires no employees." The term is used in Canadian Labor Statistics to distinguish between the single worker and the "self-employed employer" who may have one or more employees.

Partnership   A legal structure in which two or more people act as co-owners. There are many forms of partnership, including very simple ones that offer the same flexibility and simplicity of a sole proprietorship.

P.C.   Initials which do double duty for "personal computer" and "personal copier"—two items which have helped self-employed people to gain some of the benefits of the electronic revolution.
    The Canon PC-10 Cartridge Copying System, introduced in 1983, was the first office-quality copier to be sold for less than $1,000.

Perks   Slang for perquisites. The term generally refers to those special benefits that come with a job rather than those which are company-wide. Having your own washroom would be a perk, as would unlimited access to a WATS line. The self-employed person can have unlimited perks as long as there is the money to pay for them.

Personality Tests   Those examinations which ask such eternal questions as "Are you afraid of fire, the sight of blood, spiders or dirt?" and "Do you like to read 'Alice in Wonderland?'" Not being able to conform to answering these kinds of questions may keep you out of a traditional job. The issue recently got a lot of attention when psychologists hired by the Pittsburgh police department rejected 56.7% of new job applicants because they failed two standard personality tests—the Minnesota Multiphasic Personality Inventory and the Guildford-Zimmerman Temperament Survey. Needless to say, you don't have to put up with this nonsense if you are going into business for yourself.

Phillips' Law   Author's name for the principle stated in Joseph D. Phillips' 1962 book *The Self-Employed in the United States* which holds that the smaller the percentage of the working population which is self-employed the more developed the country.
    It would appear that this only works up to a point. In 1982, for instance, in Sweden and the United Kingdom the percentage of the total workforce which was self-employed was only 7% while it was 43% in Pakistan, 45% in Yemen and 28% in El Salvador. The recent rise in self-employment in the United States and other highly developed

economies would indicate, however, that there is a point in the development of a country when the percentage reverses, or, as a Labor Department economist put it, "The basic premise is nonsense."

Post-Affluence   The period of lowered living standards into which some economic forecasters think we are all headed.

Population Bulge   Academic talk for the "baby boom" which came after World War II.

Practice Control   Along with "title control," practice control is one of several new euphemisms for occupational licensing.

Private Corporation   Term used to distinguish a corporation formed by an individual from a true corporation with employees. It is a complete distortion of the term. Such corporations are designed to give the individual some of the advantages of a corporate structure and are often formed by individuals in the higher tax brackets. These individuals are technically employed by their own corporations and are counted statistically as wage and salary workers by the government. The Bureau of Labor Statistics estimated that there are more than 2,800,000 such corporations. If these people were counted as self-employed the statistics on self-employment would be significantly higher.
  One of the incentives for setting up a private corporation disappeared at the beginning of 1984 when the self-employed were given the same tax breaks in setting up pension plans which had previously only been available to the incorporated.

Pronoia   The delusion that you are doing well at work just because the boss smiles at you. The opposite of paranoia, it gets people into trouble because they think everything is fine when it isn't. This workplace peril was termed and written about by Fred Golner, a sociologist at Queens College in New York.

Quality of Work   Catchall term for a collection of new attitudes and approaches which gained ground in the workplace of the 1970s. These included creating new opportunities for people to think while they work, replacing heavy-handed supervision with greater individual responsibility for getting the job done, employee participation in decision making, giving individuals greater control over their workday schedules and redesigning jobs that have become monotonous and meaningless over time.
  Unlike other new concepts which often prescribe rigid formulas for change, the "quality of work" movement is characterized by a diverse

mix of theories, practices and rule changes. In some instances, labor and management are collaborating on questions of safety, production and hiring. Some companies are fostering the development of semi-autonomous working groups which in effect offer the amenities of a small business within a larger whole. Still others are creating opportunities for employees to better understand and take pride in what they produce, such as having auto workers test cars coming off their own assembly line. Other employers are working with ideas that would have been hard to imagine ten or 15 years ago: alternatives to the assembly line, work spaces designed by the people who work in them and new arrangements for dealing with daily work schedules.

Most of these innovations replicate to some degree the freedom which comes with self-employment or working for a small business.

Rat Race, The   Perhaps, the leading cliche associated with self-employment, as in, "I couldn't stand the rat race anymore which is why I'm doing what I am today." Runnerup: "the old grind."

Re-careering   Term used by Ronald Krannich in his book *Re-careering in Turbulent Times* to describe the strategy by which people prepare for and take on new careers. Krannich believes that high technology, the managerial glut and other factors are ganging up to doom what he terms "the one-career one-life one-job phenomenon." He feels we are moving into an era when the average person will go through several careers in a lifetime.

Recession   Statistically at least, the time of opportunity for the self-employed. William Whiston, director of economic research for the Small Business Administration, was quoted on this in the *Washington Post* in 1982; "In prosperous times people make what they know how to make. But during periods of recession and high unemployment, people scratch around for new ideas. That's when your basement inventors and new-business providers get going."

Retirement Test   For Social Security purposes, the test of whether one is truly retired and entitled to full benefits. The test is different for the self-employed. To quote a 1984 Social Security advisory, "Retired persons whose livelihood was based on self-employment should note that any income they receive that is based on services performed before entitlement to Social Security benefits is not subject to the annual limit on the amount of earnings a person may have without affecting his or her benefits." Those who benefit from this include self-employed insurance agents who get renewal commissions and those who get income from their investment in a business or partnership.

RIF   It stands for "reduction in force" and is the current government euphemism for being fired by a federal, state or local government agency. The use of the term and its verb ("riffed") have driven home the fact that job security is often a cruel illusion held by those in jobs which were once seen as good for a lifetime.

Schedule C   The Internal Revenue Service form used by unincorporated small businesses. The term is often used by the self-employed in determining if another person has incorporated or not, as in, "Are you Schedule C?"

Schmoozing   Yiddish for friendly, heart-to-heart talking. It has been used by Studs Terkel in *Working* to describe the "sense of companionship and togetherness among workers as they chat about their lives and gripe about common problems."

Self-Employment Tax   The official name for the payment which the self-employed must pay into the Social Security system. It jumped from 9.35% in 1983 to 14% in 1984 and will, under present law, rise to 15.30% in 1990. It is literally a tax on being self-employed.

Service Economy   What the United States became in April of 1982 when for the first time in history more Americans were working in service industries, finance, insurance and real estate than in manufacturing, mining and construction. This fits with the fact that self-employment is dominated by service-side jobs.

Small Business   A deceptively complex term because the govenment keeps changing the official definition of what is and what is not a small business. Presently, manufacturers and wholesalers are considered small if they employ 500 or less workers, while other businesses are judged on their annual revenues. Under the set of definitions which took hold on March 12, 1984—and which cost nearly three-quarters of a million dollars to develop—only 2% of the nation's 11 million businesses are considered "large." These definitions replace a set in which 99% of the nation's businesses were defined as small. From the standpoint of the self-employed and the truly small, small business, the term has come to refer to all but the largest companies. Phyllis Gillis, author of *Entrepreneurial Mothers*, has suggested the term "micro business" to distinguish the smallest of small business from the rest.

Social Security War   A phrase which has been tossed about to describe the potential conflict between younger workers who will be called upon to pay more and more to support the growing number of older Americans.

Sole Proprietorship   The legal/IRS term for a business owned and operated by one person. It is one of three basic structures open to the self-employed, the other two being private corporations and partnerships. Of the three, it is the easiest to form and subject to the fewest controls. However, if you get into a position where your debts are more than you can pay, your *personal* assets may have to be sold, which is not the case with a private corporation.

Stabile   One of the more recent terms used to distinguish between workers in the workplace. In this case the electrical conductance of the worker's skin is used to determine that person's suitability for a job. *Stabiles* are people with a low level of "electrodermal activity" while their opposite numbers, labiles, have skin that sends the needle high. The "human factors" people say that *labiles* are best for jobs requiring vigilance while stabiles do better in complex situations.

Steel-Collar Jobs   Name for the jobs that have been or will be usurped by industrial robots. Estimates published in the *Wall Street Journal* and other places predict as many as 120,000 robots at work by the year 2000 displacing countless blue-collar jobs. An MIT robotics expert has said, "New technology based on computers, as symbolized by robots, will be one of the—if not the—collective bargaining issues of the coming decade."

Stimulus underload   Current psychological jargon for that which is monotonous, unsatisfying and unchallenging—one of a host of reasons why people become self-employed. A decade ago stimulus underload was talked of in terms of the "blue collar blues and the white collar woes."

Telecommuter   Term coined by Jack Nilles of the University of Southern California to describe the person who works with others from home via computer hookups. Nilles predicted, in 1983, that the number of telecommuters in the United States could rise to 10 million by 1990. Presumably, before this can happen many legal restrictions on working at home will have to be lifted. It is also likely to become an issue for trade unions which generally oppose the idea on the basis that the system can be used to exploit workers. According to the *Wall Street Journal* of February 13, 1985, there were some 100,000 telecommuters at work in the United States.

"Temping"   Slang for temporary employment.

Termination at Will   The name for the principle which most employers maintain as their inalienable right: firing employees whenever and for whatever reason they deem appropriate. It is a right which has been upheld by the courts, which have denied that fired workers have "any general right of review." It is a useful term to bring up when the employed asks the self-employed person how he or she can deal with the insecurity of being self-employed.

Underground Economy   The term which has become accepted to describe that segment of the economy which sells goods and services without reporting its success to the Internal Revenue Service. Estimates as to the true size of this second economy range wildly from as low as a few billion a year to as high as $700 billion a year. A 1983 Census Bureau study commissioned by Congress concluded that a realistic estimate would be $222 billion a year, or about 7.5% of the nation's gross national product.

Other names for it include the "hidden," "unmeasured," "subterranean," and "whispering" economy. In Britain it is called the "black economy," and in France *"le travail noir."* Presumably, it is a worldwide phenomenon.

Underselfemployed   A term which begged to be created to cover that particular situation when a self-employed person is underemployed. When a self-employed person's earnings drop considerably, it has been said that the person is financing his or her own unemployment.

Videotex   Two-way information systems using television and an electronic keyboard with a vast list of potential services. It is at the core of telecommuting and the electronic cottage and effectively takes a group of existing technologies (television, communications, computer) and puts them together. A 1982 study by the Institute for the Future predicts that 40% of all American homes will be so equipped by 1998. The study also forecasts much more work at home as well as a whole new "home-based cottage industry in electronic products."

Voice to Type   Describes future office system in which a person will be able to speak to a word processor and have it display spoken words in type. It would mean, for instance, that a letter could be dictated directly into a machine, examined on a screen, corrected verbally and printed without benefit of a secretary or stenographer. It is still a drawing board idea, but several companies are working hard to develop the first such system.

A growing body of opinion states that such systems will have a tremendous impact on the white-collar labor force in the coming years, equivalent to the impact of robots on blue-collar jobs. According to David A. Hirschberg, a Small Business Administration economist, "The most profound effect may be to put large numbers of women out of work." Hirschberg believes that voice to type systems could proliferate at the rate which word processors are now doing.

Workaholic   Recently coined term for the person who is addicted to work. Ills ranging from heart attacks to divorce have been linked to it and it has been largely discussed in terms of a malady which requires treatment. A study of workaholics conducted by psychologist Marilyn Machlowitz, however, concluded that most of them were both content with their lives and happy.

Workstead   Recently coined term for living and working in the same place. It is a companion term to "homestead" used as it has been among those who have gone back to the land to operate subsistance farms. It is also the title of a book on working at home by Jeremy Joan Hewes who appears to have created the term. She wrote at the beginning of her book, "The word *workstead* slipped out of my ballpoint as I was writing a letter to a friend who moved to the country and took his work with him." Recently, it has been heard in a blend with "telecommuting" to yield the mouthful term "teleworksteading."

ACKNOWLEDGMENTS

Although the self-employed work on their own, they seldom work alone. This book underscores the point as many helped.

First and foremost, I would like to thank those who were willing to participate in *Project Watercooler* and tell me about their self-employed livelihoods. Because some of those who took part asked for anonymity, I have only listed the "public" participants in the WATERCOOLER HONOR ROLL which follows. I would also like to thank the editors of several magazines and newsletters which helped me find people to question by writing about *Project Watercooler.* These are *In Business, Creative Living* and *The Crafts Report.*

I would also like to thank several self-employed writers who let me use them to discuss and refine ideas on the subject at hand. These people are Dan Rapoport, Bob Skole, William Mead and Joseph C. Goulden.

A select group of people within the government were especially helpful in helping me find and interpret information and statistics on self-employment. They are:

Congressional Reference Service—Marvin Kornbluh
General Accounting Office—Pat Tyson
Internal Revenue Service—Berj Kenadjian
                   Ray Wolf
Labor Department—Ron Whiting
                   Deborah Klein
                   Gail Martin
                   Tom Nardone
                   Eugene Becker
Small Business Administration—David A. Hirschberg
                   Bruce D. Phillips
Social Security Administration—Myra Williams

I would also like to thank Lane Jennings of the World Future Society, Lee Bellinger of the Center on National Labor Policy, Coralee

Kern of the National Association for the Cottage Industry, and Wayne Boucher for their help.

Lastly, I would like to thank all those who enlisted in *Project Watercooler*. They are:

Katherine Ackerman, Christine Adamec, Robert Anderson, Max Aquilera-Hellweg.

Jane H. Bailey, Nathaniel Barrows, Ed Bashaw, Shirley Baxter, Shari Bellamy, Mary Ann Bergeron, Louise Borquez, Bruce Boston, V. Arthur Bova, Jr., Katherene Brehm, Sarah Anne Brite, Dick Brown, Tafi Brown, Danny Buelk, Fred Burnham, Terry L. Burrington, Patrick Butler.

Jim Cameron, Dan Capell, Judy Casaroli, Bill Casey, Barb Cash, James P. Clark, Charisma Clay, Carole Coffelt, Edward B. Cone, Janet M. Conley, Anna Coombes, Stephen D. Cooper, Alyce P. Cornyn-Selby, John S. Craig, Les Crawley, Jack Crittenden, Walter H. Croft.

Dorothy Daly, Gary Davisson, Darlene, Sylvia DeLong, J.R. DeMonte, Alfred deQuoy, Dick DeRoy, Rowena Dery.

Robert Ebstein, Noelle El-Negoumy.

Jan Fazio, Carol Feierabend, Rick Fogg, Jim Forgus, Judi Friedman, Helen Fushetto.

Neil Garvin, Marcy Gates, Dilip Gohil, Marc Goldring, Daniel W. Gottlieb, Joseph C. Goulden, Jim Graham, Franklin Gray, Rich Gregory, Michael Greon, Elizabeth A. Grindle, Pat Grossman.

Mary Alice Hearn, Eugenia Hershenson, William Curt Hess, Marty Higgs, Marybeth Highton, Robert M. Hodies, Elizabeth Holster.

Lori Jean Karluk, Eva Kataja, Klamon, Edward M. Kolbe, Jr., John Paul Kowal, Romany Kramaris, Dawn Krick, R. J. Krueger,

Hallinan Lagan, Jeffrey Lant, Lori Leohr, Arthur Lind, Alfred Lockwood, Edward Lorenzen, Kelly Lukes.

Cynthia Macgregor, Arthur Magida, Mariel, Betty Marshall, Charles Marshall, Donna Martin, Morris McClellan, Giorgetta McRee, Carole Meola, Karen Meyers, Steve Mihaly, Robert Montague, Frank Moran, Peg Moran, T.C. Moran, George Taylor Morris, Christopher Morrow, Liz Myers.

Jan W. Nahorski, Bob North, Hank Nuwer.

Joann M. Olstrom.

Cindy Pacileo, Dennis Panke, Louis Phillips, Richard Pierce, Levi Pleshe, Melinda Pleshe, Philip L. Pollack, Ann Powell-Brown, Dan Poynter, Jim Price, Joyce Price.

Caroline Rackley, Jim Randall, Dave Raymond, Elisavietta Ritchie, Robert of Word Power Inc., Caroline Roper-Deyo, O. Shannon Russell.

Scott Saari, John Salony, Charles Salzberg, Ann Scharff, Joann Schmidt, Bob Schulman, Virginia Schulte, Caryl Simpson, Tim Sims, Jules Skoletsky, Barcine Smith, Michael Smith, Hal Speer, Saul A. Stadmauer, Penelope Comfort Starr, Arline Stephenson, Paul Stroessels, Murray Suid.

Roy Thorne, Brook Trout, Michele Tuegel.

Bill Valentine, Kevin Van Gundy, Marsha Vander-Heyden, Vincent A. van Haaff.

Richard P. Warren, Tom Warrner, D. Michael Werner, Paul Wesel, Hilde Weisert, Mike Whelan, Tony Wightman, Roger Wilken, Paul Wittstock, Louise Woerner, D.K. Wolfe, Arthur Wolfson, Charlotte Wood.

Mark Zilliox, Barbara Zimmerman, Isaiah M. Zimmerman.

As this book goes to press, I am still getting letters and notes from people who want to participate in *Project Watercooler*. I will keep gathering information on the self-employed species which will come in handy should there be a demand for future editions of this book. If any of you wish to write to me about your self-employment or should you want a *Watercooler* questionnaire, feel free to write to me care of:

PROJECT WATERCOOLER
Box 80
Garrett Park, MD 20896

BIBLIOGRAPHY

This is not meant to be a comprehensive bibliography citing every single article and report consulted but rather one which points to the sources which I think would be most useful to people thinking about self-employment and the general nature of working. I've noted those which I think are particularly useful.

Amara, Roy. *The Future of Management: Ten Shapers of Management in the 1980s.* Menlo Park, Calif.: The Institute for the Future, 1980.

Anreder, Steven S. *Retirement Dollars for the Self-Employed.* New York: Thomas Y. Crowell, 1972.

Applegath, John. *Working Free.* New York: AMACOM, 1982.

Bailey, Geoffrey. *Maverick: Succeeding as a Free-Lance Entrepreneur.* New York: Franklin Watts, 1982.

Basi, Bart A., and Earlin, David L. *The Corporate Form of Business and the Self-Employed.* State College, Center for Research of the College of Business Administration, Pennsylvania State University, 1975.

Becker, Eugene H. "Self-Employed Workers: an Update to 1983." *Monthly Labor Review.* July 1984.

Best, Fred. *The Future of Work.* Englewood Cliffs, N.J.: Prentice-Hall, 1973.

Biggs, Don. *Breaking Out.* New York: David McKay Co., 1973.

Birch, David L. *The Job Generation Process.* Cambridge, Mass.: MIT Program on Neighborhood and Regional Change, 1979.
   This book first established the fact that small business was more likely to create new jobs than big business. The kind of firm most likely to create jobs was "small", "independent" and "volatile," according to Birch. The book helped create a new picture of small business and entrepreneurship.

Bolles, Richard Nelson. *What Color is Your Parachute?* Berkeley, Calif: Ten Speed Press, 1972.

Bregger, John E. "Self-Employment in the United States, 1948-62." *Monthly Labor Review,* January 1963.

Brown, Deaver. *The Entrepreneur's Guide.* New York: Macmillan, 1980.

Burns, Scott. *Home Inc: The Hidden Wealth and Power of the American Household.* Garden City, N.Y.: Doubleday, 1975.

Butz, W.P., McCarthy, P., Morrison, P.A., and Vaiana, M.E. *Demographic Challenges in America's Future.* Santa Monica: RAND Corp., 1982.
Useful and fascinating distillation of the demographic trends likely to have the greatest impact in the next few decades.

Campbell, Rita Ricardo. *Social Security: Promise and Reality.* Stanford, Calif.: Hoover Institute Press, 1977.
Must reading for anyone trying to unravel the history of Social Security reform.

Camden, Thomas M. *A Language Guide to Outplacement.* Hinsdale, Ill.: Camden and Associates, 1981.

Carlson, Richard C., et al. *Energy Futures, Human Values and Lifestyles.* Boulder: Westview Press, 1982.

Cetron, Marvin, and O'Toole, Thomas. *Encounters with the Future: A Forecast of Life into the 21st Century.* New York: McGraw-Hill, 1982.

Changing Times. "Getting the Jump on Tomorrow's Jobs." August 1983.
—."Running a Business at Home: How to Get It Going." February 1983.

Cook, Peter D. *Start and Run Your Own Successful Business.* New York: Beaufort, 1982.

Cornish, Edward, ed. *Careers Tomorrow.* Bethesda, Md: World Future Society, 1983.
A rich sampling of futurist thinking on the subject of work.

Cornuelle, Richard. *De-Managing America: The Final Revolution.* New York: Random House, 1975.
One of several books which looked at the dark side of bureaucratic control and traditional management. It became gospel for those sick of the boss and his rules.

Cowen, Robert. "Cottage Computing: Glorifying the Trivial?" *Technology Review,* November/December 1981.

Cox, Alan. *The Cox Report on the American Corporation*. New York: Delacorte Press, 1982.
Compelling report on what it takes to get to the top of the corporate ladder.

Crichton, Michael. *Electronic Life*. New York: Knopf, 1983.

Davidson, Peter. *Earn Money at Home*. New York: McGraw-Hill, 1982.

Deken, Joseph. *The Electronic Cottage*. New York: Bantam Books, 1983.

Delany, George, and Delany, Sandra. *The #1 Home Business Book*. Cockeysville, Md: Liberty Publishing, 1981.

Dible, Donald M., *Up Your Own Organization!* Santa Clara: Entrepreneur Press, 1971.

Didsbury, Howard F., Jr., ed. *The World of Work: Careers and the Future*. Bethesda: World Future Society, 1983.
Papers presented at the World Future Society's 1983 conference on "Work Now and in the Future." Recommended for anyone who wants to think about the future of work.

Dodd, James B. "Information Brokers." *Special Libraries*, May/June 1976.

Ellis, John. *The New Financial Guide for the Self-Employed*. Chicago: Contemporary Books, 1981.

Fain, T. Scott. "Self-Employed Americans: Their Number Has Increased." *Monthly Labor Review*, November 1980.

Faux, Marian. *Successful Freelancing*. New York: St. Martin's Press, 1982.

Feingold, Norman, and Perlman, Leonard. *Making It On Your Own*. Washington, D.C.: Acropolis Books, 1981.

Feldstein, Stuart. *Home, Inc*. New York: Grosset and Dunlap, 1981.

Fullerton, Howard N., and Tschetter, John. "The 1995 Labor Force: A Second Look." *Monthly Labor Review*, November 1983.

Galbraith, John Kenneth. *Economics and the Public Purpose*. Boston: Houghton, Mifflin, 1973.
One of those books of the last decade which told us that small, independent business was "an anachronism."

Ginzberg, Eli; Mills, Daniel Quinn; Owen, John D.; Sheppard, Harold L.; and Wachter, Michael L. *Work Decisions in the 1980s*. Boston: Auburn House Publishing, 1982.

Goldstein, Jerome. *In Business for Yourself*. New York: Charles Scribner's Sons, 1982.

Graebner, William. *A History of Retirement: The Meaning and Function of an American Institution*. New Haven: Yale University Press, 1982.

Gumpert, David E., and Timmons, Jeffry A. *The Insider's Guide to Small Business Resources*. New York: Doubleday, 1981.
The best directory for the small operator. Hundreds of sources of financial help and information are amply explained and discussed.

Gray, Thomas A., and Hirschberg, David A. *Shifts in the Employment Status of Proprietors, 1960-1975*. U.S. Small Business Administration, Office of Advocacy, 1983.

Gyllenhammar, Pehr G. *People at Work*. Reading, Mass.: Addison-Wesley, 1977.

Health, Education and Welfare, U.S. Department of. *Work in America*. Cambridge, Mass.: MIT Press, 1973.

Hewitt, Geof. *Working for Yourself*. Emmaus, Pa.: Rodale Press, 1977.

Hewes, Jeremy Joan. *Worksteads: Living and Working in the Same Place*. Garden City, N.Y.: Doubleday/Dolphin, 1983.

International Labor Organization. *1982 Year Book of Labour Statistics*. Geneva: International Labor Office, 1983.

Jones, Landon Y. *Great Expectations: America and the Baby Boom Generation*. New York: Coward, McCann and Geoghegan, 1980.

Jones, Tony. "The New Anatomy." *Creative Living*, Summer 1983.

Jorgenson, James. *The Graying of Amerrca: Retirement and Why You Can't Afford it*. New York: Dial, 1982.
—. *Your Retirement Income*. New York: Charles Scribner's Sons, 1982.
Journal of Career Education. "A Special Issue on Entrepreneurship Education." December 1981.

Kahn, Herman, and Wiener, Anthony J. *The Year 2000*. New York: Macmillan, 1967.
The book that told us that in the year 2000 seeking a vocation would be labeled "selfish, excessively narrow or compulsive."

Kanter, Rosabeth Moss. "A Good Job is Hard to Find." *Working Papers*, May/June 1979.

Kellog, Mary Alice. *Fast Track: The Superachievers and How They Make It to Early Success, Status and Power.* New York: McGraw-Hill, 1978.

Kerr, Clark, and Rosow, Jerome M. *Work in America: The Decade Ahead.* New York: Van Nostrand Reinhold, 1979.

Kornbluh, Marvin. *New Technology in the American Workplace.* Washington, D.C.: Library of Congress, Congressional Research Service, 1983.

Krannich, Ronald L. *Re-Careering in Turbulent Times.* Manassas, Va.: Impact, 1983.

Lefkowitz, Bernard. *Breaktime.* New York: Hawthorne Books, 1979.
The book that dared to discuss the option of not working.

Leveson, Irving. "Some Determinants of Nonfarm Self-Employment." *Monthly Labor Review*, May 1968.

Levitt, Arthur, Jr. "In Praise of Small Business." *New York Times Magazine,* December 6, 1981.

Levy, Marcia. *Self-Employment in the Covered Workforce*, Washington D.C.: U.S. Department of Health, Education and Welfare, Social Security Administration, Office of Research and Statistics, 1975.
One of the only attempts the government has made to analyze working independence. Fascinating because it analyzes the statistics gathered when self-employment was at rock bottom.

Lohr, Steve. "Small Business: Job Role Highlighted." *New York Times*, January 18, 1980.
—."Small Business: Working Its Way Out of Federal Neglect." *New York Times*, February 24, 1980.

Long, Larry, and DeAre, Diana. "The Slowing of Urbanization in the US." *Scientific American*, July 1983.

Lowrey, Albert J. *How to Become Financially Successful by Owning Your Own Business.* New York: Simon and Schuster, 1981.

McCaslin, Barbara S., and McNamara, Patricia P. *Be Your Own Boss: A Woman's Guide to Planning and Running Her Business.* Englewood Cliffs, N.J.: Prentice-Hall, 1980.

Maccoby, Michael. *The Gamesman.* New York: Simon and Schuster, 1976.

Mancuso, Joseph. *Fun and Guts, the Entrepreneur's Philosophy.* Reading, Mass.: Addison-Wesley, 1973.
—. *Small Business Survival Guide.* Englewood Cliffs, N.J.: Prentice-Hall, 1980.
A yellow pages for the self-employed and small-business owner listing more than 700 sources of available capital.

Matthews, Kathy. *On Your Own: 99 Alternatives to a 9-to-5 Job.* New York: Vintage Books, 1977.
More than any other book, this one displayed the new attitude that said there are no limits to an independent livelihood. Impractical notions aside (treasure hunting and bumper-sticker writing, to name two) it was the perfect antidote to the litany that the only option we had was corporate, "grown up" work.

Moran, Peg. *Invest in Yourself.* Rohnert Park, Calif.: Upstream Press, 1982.

Myers, Robert D. *Social Security.* 2nd ed. Bryn Mawr, Pa.: McCahan Foundation, 1981.

Naisbitt, John. *Megatrends.* New York: Warner Books, 1982.

Nilles, Jack. "Teleworking: Working Closer to Home." *Technology Review,* April 1982.
One of several articles in which Nilles paints a rosy picture for the future of telecommuting.

Norman, Colin. "Microelectronics at Work: Productivity and Jobs in the World Economy." *Worldwatch Paper #39.* Washington, D.C.: Worldwatch Institute, 1980.

O'Toole, James; Scheiber, Jane L.; and Wood, Linda C. *Working Changes and Choices.* New York: Human Sciences Press, 1981.

Phillips, Bruce D. "The Marketing of Small Business by Big Business." Unpublished paper by a senior economist at the Small Business Administration.
Big business is learning, says Phillips, that it is increasingly dependent on small firms and independent contractors for innovation, job creation and, above all, customers.

Phillips, Joseph D. *The Self-Employed in the United States.* Urbana: University of Illinois, 1962.
The only major academic study of the self-employed in the United States. Phillips found a dwindling self-employed workforce which was increasingly composed of older men and handicapped workers who were the rejects of the corporate culture. Must reading for anyone who wants to fully appreciate the changes in the self-employed workforce.

Phillips, Michael, and Raspberry, Salli. *Honest Business: A Superior Strategy for Starting and Managing Your Own Business.* San Francisco: Clear Glass Publishing Co., 1981.

Ray, Robert. "A Report on Self-Employed Americans in 1973." *Monthly Labor Review,* January 1975.

Roby, Pamela. *Women in the Workplace.* Cambridge, Mass.: Schenkman Publishing, 1981.

Rowley, Nora P. "Want to be Your Own Boss?" *Occupational Outlook Quarterly,* February 1965.

Russell, Louise B. "The Baby Boom Generation and the Labor Market in the Next Decade." *World Future Society Bulletin,* November/December 1983.

Schiff, Frank W. *Looking Ahead: Identifying Key Economic Issues for Business and Society in the 1980s.* New York: Committee for Economic Development, 1980.

Shapero, Albert. "Numbers That Lie." *Inc.,* May 1981.
A devastating attack on the myth that almost all new enterprises fail within a short time.

Sheppard, Harold L., and Herrick, Neal Q. *Where Have All the Robots Gone?* New York: Free Press, 1972.
Still stands as the great study of worker dissatisfaction and satisfaction.

Shilling, Dana. *Be Your Own Boss.* New York: Morrow, 1983.

Shimberg, Benjamin; Esser, Barbara F.; and Kruger, Daniel H. *Occupational Licensing: Practices and Policies.* Washington, D.C.: Public Affairs Press, 1973.

Smith, Brian. *How to Prosper in Your Own Business.* Brattleboro, Vt.: Stephen Greene Press, 1981.

Smith, Irene. *Diary of a Small Business.* New York: Charles Scribner's Sons, 1983.

Smith, Randy Baca. *Setting Up Shop: The Do's and Don'ts of Starting a Small Business.* New York: Warner Books, 1983.

Spates, Thomas G. *Human Values Where People Work.* New York: Harper and Brothers, 1960.

Stein, Leon. *Out of the Sweatshop.* New York: New York Times Books, 1978.
Must reading for anyone wanting to understand why organized labor is so deeply opposed to homework.

Stickney, John. *Self-Made: Braving an Independent Career in a Corporate Age.* New York: G.P. Putnam's Sons, 1980.
Extended profiles of self-employed Americans. More than any other recent books it captures the true spirit of the urge.

Taylor, Frederick Winslow. *The Principles of Scientific Management*. New York: Harper and Brothers, 1911.
  Still an eye-opener for its unintended ability to tell us what is wrong with the 20th century workplace.

Tepper, Terri P., and Tepper, Nona Dawe. *The New Entrepreneurs: Women Working from Home*. New York: Universe Books, 1980.

Terkel, Studs. *Working*. New York: Pantheon Books, 1974.

Toffler, Alvin. *Future Shock*. New York: Random House, 1970.
—. *Previews and Premises*. New York: Morrow, 1983.
—. *The Third Wave*. New York: Morrow, 1980.
  Toffler is required reading for anyone who wants to seriously think about the future. Of these three *The Third Wave* has the greatest bearing on self-employment.

Toner, William. *Planning for Home Occupations*. Chicago: American Society of Planning Officials, 1976.
  Extremely useful for those grappling with local rules and regulations concerning work at home.

Tuccile, Jerome. *Inside the Underground Ecomony*. New York: New American Library, 1982.

Tydeman, J.; Lipinski, H.; Adler, R.; Nyhan, M.; and Zwimpfer, L. *Teletext and Videotex in the United States*. New York: McGraw-Hill, 1982.
  Dense, meaty study on the future impact of electronics at home and at work.

U.S. Comptroller General. *Tax Treatment of Employees and Self-Employed Persons by the Internal Revenue Service: Problems and Solutions*. Washington, D.C.: Government Printing Office, 1977.

U.S. Department of Labor, Bureau of Labor Statistics. *Economic Projections to 1990*. Washington, D.C.: GPO, 1982.
—. *Occupational Outlook Handbook*. Washington, D.C.: GPO, 1982.

U.S. General Accounting Office. *IRS Needs to Curb Excessive Deductions for Self-Employment Retirement Plans*. Washington, D.C.: GPO, 1982.

U.S. House of Representatives, Committee on Science and Technology, Subcommittee on Investigations and Oversight. *Job Forecasting*. Washington, D.C.: GPO, 1983.
—. Committee on Ways and Means, Subcommittee on Health. *Proceedings of the Conference on the Future of Medicare*. Washington, D.C.: GPO, 1984.
—. Committee on Ways and Means, Subcommittee on Social Security. *Financing Problems of the Social Security System*. Washington, D.C.: GPO, 1983.

—. Committee on Ways and Means, Subcommittee on Select Revenue Measures. *Independent Contractors.* Washington, D.C.: GPO, 1979.

U.S. Internal Revenue Service. *Business Income Tax Returns: Sole Proprietorships, Partnerships.* Washington D.C.: Government Printing Office, 1979, 1980, etc.
—. *Individual Income Tax Returns.* Washington, D.C.: Government Printing Office, 1979, 1980, etc.

U.S. Senate, Committee on Finance. *Self-Employed Individuals Retirement Act.* Hearings of 1959 and 1961. Washington, D.C.: Government Printing Office, 1959 and 1961.
Fascinating reading today as they reveal the extent to which the Treasury Department and other parts of official Washington feared the fiscal impact of Keogh plans.
—. Committee on Small Business. *Small Business Issues and Priorities—1983.* Washington, D.C.: GPO, 1983.
Contains important background on the new self-employment tax.

U.S. Small Business Administration. *The State of Small Business: A Report of the President.* Washington, D.C.: Government Printing Office, reports of 1982, 1983, 1984.
The closest thing that there is to an annual report on the state of small enterprise in America. Published each March. The 1984 report is of particular importance because it shows the "disproportionate" role that the self-employed have had in the recovery from the 1980-1982 recession. Unlike most government reports, this one seems to get better by the year.

Vesper, Karl. *Entrepreneurship and National Policy.* Chicago: Heller Institute for Small Business, 1983.

White, Theodore H. *America in Search of Itself.* New York: Harper and Row, 1982.
This book contains a remarkably fact-filled section on what the 1980 Census has told us about ourselves.

Whittlesey, Marietta. *Freelance Forever: Successful Self-Employment.* New York: Avon Books, 1982.
A particularly useful book for writers, artists and others in the arts. I hope that this book continues to be published in updated editions.

Whyte, William H. *The Organization Man.* New York: Simon and Schuster, 1956.

Work in America Institute. *New Work Schedules for a Changing Society.* Scarsdale, N.Y.: Work in America Institute, 1981.

Yankelovich, Daniel. *New Rules: Searching for Self-Fulfillment in a World Turned Upside Down.* New York: Bantam Books, 1982.
   Especially interesting on the subject of risks and why we seem willing to take them.
— and Immerwahr, John. "Putting the Work Ethic to Work." *Technology Review*, November/December 1983.

Periodicals for The Self-Employed

There are several magazines and newsletters which are particularly useful to the self-employed.

The Crafts Report. Should be read by all those who are self-employed and in the business of handicrafts. Address: 3632 Ashworth North, Seattle, Wash. 98103.

In Business. Monthly magazine for the smaller of small businesses. For the self-employed individual it is probably the most useful of all the business magazines. Address: Box 323, 18 South Seventh St., Emmaus, Pa. 18049.

Mind Your Own Business at Home. Newletter from Coralee S. Kern and the National Association for the Cottage Industry. It covers such matters as zoning, licensing, taxes and legal information. Address: P.O. Box 14850, Chicago, Ill. 60614.

Profitline: The Newsletter of the National Association for the Self-Employed. Despite the name, this group tends to be more interested in small business management than in the solitary operator, but its newletter covers much that is of interest. Address: NASE, P.O. Box 612067, Dallas/Fort Worth, Texas 75261.

INDEX